what are
children
for?

what are children for?

Laurie Taylor & Matthew Taylor

With research assistance by Anna Lodge

 SHORT BOOKS

First published in 2003 by

Short Books

15 Highbury Terrace

London N5 1UP

10 9 8 7 6 5 4 3 2 1

Copyright ©

Laurie Taylor and Matthew Taylor 2003

A CIP catalogue record for this book

is available from the British Library.

ISBN 1-904095-25-9

Printed in Great Britain by

Bookmarque Ltd, Croydon, Surrey

For Joe and Cornell and Cathie and Claire

first words

This short book was prompted by a conversation with my son. We were out drinking together and had reached that point in the evening, familiar no doubt to other fathers and sons, when we both vaguely sensed the need to get away from the usual mundane chatter about football and work and say something, however stumbling and incoherent, about what we meant to each other. We talked about how pleasant it was that we could now drink together without resorting to the mutual recriminations that had dogged our earlier relationship. We talked about how much we now had in common and how much we had slowly developed a grudging respect for each other's rather different lifestyles.

It was at this moment that Matthew asked, in a matter-of-fact tone, if I could answer a question that had been troubling him for some time. Why was it, he wondered, that I had so rarely shown any enthusiasm for my role as his father. Why had I so persistently shied away from being a proper or a normal dad?'

I explained as patiently as I could that I had never wanted to be a conventional father. Neither had I been alone. Matthew's mother, despite the many sacrifices she had made while bringing Matthew up on her own, had been equally unready to adopt a traditional maternal role. But this was not, for either of us, solely a matter of biography: it was also an ideological choice. Many of the parents we knew back in the Sixties shared the view that to regard one's child as some sort of educational or occupational project was thoroughly reactionary. Children were to be left to create their own life, follow their own passions. If that meant that they ended up as a carpenter or an itinerant hippie, then so be it. Didn't Matthew have somewhat similar feelings about his own two small children?

No, he told me, he did not. He strongly believed that his own children needed security and unilateral love and he was determined to do his best to make sure that this was what they got. It was, he explained, quite the opposite of my approach to fatherhood. As far as he was concerned, my libertarian approach to fathering boiled down to little more than a rationalisation which gave me the license to ignore his needs and thoughtlessly pursue my own. What other explanation could there be for my constant moves around the country, my serial philandering? 'Now that I'm a father myself, I'm determined not to go down that particular road. I want to experience through my children a childhood that I didn't have myself. I want to give them one home, one school, one coherent life.'

It was a fine speech. How could I be anything but embarrassed by the contrast that Matthew had drawn between his commitment to his children and my own behaviour towards him? But I had a question of my own that I knew might cause him equal concern. Why, I wondered, had there been so many occasions when I'd seen him in the depths of despair about his role as parent and family man?

He immediately admitted that it was true that his attempts to be a better parent were often bedevilled by the sense that he was personally deriving little benefit or value from his sacrifices. Too often he found himself looking at friends and childless colleagues and envying them their freedom, their lack of responsibilities, their full and exciting lives. In his bleaker moments he asked himself the question that he had originally put to me: What are children for?

After that evening we found ourselves trying to resolve the issues our conversation had raised by putting the same question to friends and colleagues who either had children or had decided to remain child-free. It was their answers that eventually formed the basis of an article which we wrote for the British journal of ideas, *Prospect*. The response to this piece surprised us both. Many of our critics objected strongly to our question. How dare we talk about children as though they had a use-value like a new vacuum cleaner? Many others wrote and e-mailed to say that we had ignored this or that absolutely obvious reason for having and for loving children. It was clear that we had touched a nerve.

This was all the encouragement we needed. For the next six months, whenever we found ourselves in a position to set the conversational agenda (in coffee bars, over dinner tables, at conferences and seminars), we returned to our question. This was not a systematic or a controlled study. We confined ourselves to middle-class parents, prospective parents, grandparents and the child-free because these were the people that we knew best, and also because it seemed to us that it is within this section of society that the most passionate debates about child-bearing and child-rearing are located. There was, though, another justification for restricting our sample in this way. Everything we read in the literature about changing attitudes towards children suggested that there is a filter-down effect. Views that are held by the middle classes in one generation are highly likely to be adopted by less privileged sections of society in the next. A very similar justification informed our decision to confine our questions to the white middle class. The most recent research into the family structures and child-bearing patterns of the main ethnic minority groups in Britain suggests that, despite current variations, all are moving, in terms of both attitudes and behaviour towards children, in the same direction as the indigenous white population.

These conversations convinced us of one thing. Child-bearing and child-rearing have indeed become highly problematic. Activities that were once taken more or less for granted (even if often beset by ill health and premature death) are now arousing profound doubts and uncertainties. They have become highly contentious.

There is, of course, one straightforward reason for this new state of affairs. Modern methods of birth control have created the possibility for all children to be chosen. Children are in theory, even if not always in practice, optional: every child can now be a wanted child. But what exactly is a wanted child? How does one balance such a want for a child against the pull of career and good times? What are the costs and the risks of having children? What difference will a child make to my life? What will my child mean to me when he or she grows older? How might I explain my decision to remain 'child-free' to others in ways that would meet with their approval? How can I justify my complaints about the frustrations of child-rearing when my children have been freely chosen?

The more we talked, the more we realised that there is one great obstacle to resolving these debates. While we have begun to dispense with traditional stories about the meaning of children in our lives, we have not, as yet, developed any other accounts that will provide plausible explanations for our current dilemmas and predicaments. Our freedom to choose has not simultaneously provided us with the means to make sense of our choices.

Such stories and narratives are critical to our sense of well-being. Although we may talk about 'planning' our children, we rarely make decisions to have children, or to remain child-free, or to postpone having children until later in life, according to the strict rationalist criteria that we might bring to bear upon choices about moving house or changing jobs. Not only do judicious calculations seem out of place in relation to such intensely personal and emotional choices, but it is also extremely difficult to calculate the long-term implications of our decisions in this area of life. The problem with children, as we were frequently told, is that they last an awfully long time!

This means that we can only make sense of our decisions to have children, or our frustration at trying to reconcile their presence with our own investment in career or self-expression, by listening to what our friends and colleagues have to say about such matters. How do they explain their distinctive choices? What stories provide them with personal comfort? And reassurance?

These stories are not merely justifications. Our decisions about whether to have children or to remain child-free or to postpone child-bearing, are heavily influenced by our anticipation of how others will view our choices. The guilt, for example, that is often visited upon those who choose to pursue a child-free career path can only be dissipated by the ready availability of stories that positively celebrate such career-mindedness, stories that attribute 'real' selfishness to those women who continue to procreate in an already over-populated world.

The problem for many people is that these stories are so new that they lack persuasive power. We talked to men and women who found it difficult even to discuss their ambivalent feelings about children. They realised that there was now something hollow about the traditional justification for having children but found themselves looking round in vain for new stories that might serve as an adequate replacement. One woman told us that she was 'lost for words': she desperately wanted to talk to her friends and colleagues about what a baby might mean to her but somehow could never find either the right moment or the right phrase.

This book then is primarily about how we seek, and often fail, to make sense of our decisions about children. We do not wish to claim that the conclusions we reach as a result of such limited research are in any way definitive. What we do feel confident about, though, is that our simple question – what are children for? – prompts important reflections not only on the role and status of children in our society but also on the way we live now and might choose to live in the future.

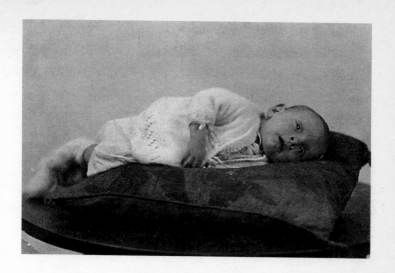

taboos and tribes

Laurie. *I have to tell you that all your talk about wanting to be a better father than me can be terribly irritating. It's an argument that I can't win. If I don't show any affection for my grandchildren, then you can write me off as some sort of emotional retard; but if I do get down on my hands and knees and play with them, you can start complaining all over again about how I never lavished any such affection on you.*

Matthew. *But you do end up winning. You have another card up your sleeve. And you can't resist playing it. You use my new status as a father to make me feel inadequate.*

One particular occasion always sticks in my head. I remember arriving one morning at your house with the family in tow. We were in our usual state – hassled, dishevelled, carrying changing-mat, nappies and toys, with moaning toddlers in tow. You met us at the door with your 'child-free' best friends who were roughly my age but unlike Claire and me were looking immaculate with their trendy clothes and suntans from a winter holiday. They'd been able to fully recover from the previous night's excesses by having a long lie-in and a leisurely morning. I realised you had invited them a day earlier so you could have some fun before the 'glums' arrived.

Laurie. *Maybe that explains why I felt your very demeanour on the doorstep was accusing, an implied rebuke to my failure to be a good father, and to the shallow hedonism of my friends. If you did feel excluded it was mainly because you were hard at work as usual turning your family into a political statement.*

***

We expected that people would disagree with our *Prospect* article about parents and children. In truth, we rather hoped to generate a debate. What took us by surprise, however, was the view that it was inappropriate for us to have even raised the question.

Among our friends and colleagues, this was in part a judgement on us. Even though we had sought to wear our most obvious failings on our sleeves, some clearly felt our own record as fathers and partners invalidated our opinions or should at least prompt a decent reticence. We were hardly being singled out. As any public figure knows, to talk about families is a perilous business unless your own is improbably perfect. This tends to inhibit or impoverish any public debate about the family: the quality of argument is judged not by its intellectual coherence but by the psychology, morality and thus 'legitimacy' of its author.

From a political perspective there was also the view that men – particularly men without any professional status in the field – should not write about what is fundamentally a woman's choice. Women bear children, and women are culturally expected (and required) to take the primary responsibility for their care. At the Institute of Public Policy Research, Matthew (the director) was sent an e-mail by a female colleague: 'Even though we have decided to forgive you, you should know just how pissed off women here were with that piece in *Prospect*.'

In subsequent conversations, it became clear that while there was a gender dimension to this irritation there was something else at issue. Each of us – whether or not we have children – has a different life story to tell. These stories, often painful, often full of regrets, feel personal and unique. There are sentiments and experiences we find hard to talk about; maybe some that we find hard to acknowledge even to ourselves. We may reluctantly admit that we fit into some category or other, for example 'childless woman over 30', but we still want to protest that we are subtly different from the average.

We should have been more prescient. Anyone who seeks to describe what happens in families must accept from the outset that their accounts can never do justice to the specificity and fine texture of real lives and relationships.

Yet there are plenty of public conversations about children. The anxieties of parents are a staple ingredient of advice columns, daytime television shows and childcare manuals. Much of this output takes the form of experts advising parents on what they should or should not do to bring up their children safely, responsibly and successfully. A large proportion of these pronouncements is pious in tone and based on dubious scientific findings, but nothing, it seems, can stem the tide.

There is little evidence that such public 'child-mongering' provides real reassurance to worried parents. Indeed, as Frank Furedi has convincingly argued, in his recent book, *Paranoid Parenting*, advice on how to cope with the anxieties of parenting has become an important source of that very anxiety. Parents may start out trying to do what they are advised, but visit the home of any parent of a young child and the odds are that you will discover a baby and toddler manual heavily thumbed up to about page 50, but strangely untouched thereafter. For Furedi, the tide of advice to parents both reinforces and is legitimised by 'the myth of parental determinism'. This is the idea that every act of the parent – from spousal conflict to cooking with E-numbers – has profound consequences for the development of their child. Sometimes it seems that every new day brings fresh evidence of how children's later delinquency, drug addiction and academic failure can be traced to yet another form of parental inadequacy.

But alongside the story of parental omnipotence, there is the quite different narrative about the parent as victim. In this account, parents are pictured as beset by a hostile world of uncaring employers, unscrupulous vendors, and unspeakable abusers. In the face of such threats, parents are left feeling that there is little if anything they can do to preserve their own child's innocence or integrity.

This, too, is a seriously distorted view of the actual nature of parenting. As we will show later, the common assertion that bringing up children is, in an objective sense, becoming costlier, more onerous and riskier, has little historical justification. We need to get beyond the fatalistic story that parents are either totally responsible for their children's destiny, or victims of a society and culture that have taken away the means that might allow that responsibility to be exercised, and to recognise that it is not so much the actual conditions of parenting that have changed but rather the manner in which we now seek to reconcile the fact of having (or indeed, not having) children with our own contemporary needs and desires. In other words, it may not be children themselves that have changed and become more problematic but our attitudes towards them.

The response to this apparent crisis in child-bearing and child-rearing needs to be two-fold. In the first place we must endeavour to locate the root causes of such ambiguity and uncertainty. To do this we need to probe the traditional reasons that were given for having children and attempt to show the ways in which these may have lost their power and credibility, their hold over our imagination. But our task does not stop there. We must also provide new stories or narratives about the meaning of children in our society that provide genuine reassurance and real comfort to both parents and non-parents. We need to rewrite the stories that we tell ourselves about ourselves.

What makes this task so urgent is the evidence that the absence of satisfactory narratives about the meaning of children has opened the gates to a new form of tribalism. Behind the modern etiquette of respect for the choices of others and sympathy for their circumstances, there are growing signs of intolerance and polarisation. On the horizon two opposing forces are gathering – those with children, and those who have chosen, at least so far, to remain child-free. The size of the second tribe has given it, for the first time in history, critical mass as a social and political force. Between these tribes there is a growing lack of communication. We feel fairly secure in saying to parents and non-parents alike that, generally speaking, you do not tell each other the truth. You do not come clean about your feelings towards each other.

It is not difficult to understand why those with children tend to see the childless as tragic failures or shallow hedonists. Parents – however bleakly they might view their own situation – find it difficult to regard childlessness as a chosen and fulfilled state. The deeply held assumption (if anything, reinforced by the ambivalence felt by parents about their own status) is that parenting is the norm and that non-parenting must therefore have some sort of pathological foundation. Parents also question the right of non-parents to make decisions or have opinions about those matters that affect children. Non-parents in positions of power frequently face the charge that they lack empathy with the predicament faced by ordinary families. They find themselves described as unfeeling and even vindictive towards those who are living what many politicians and moralists would still wish to describe as 'a normal family life'. Perhaps it is not surprising that the happy family – preferably with small children included – has become a valued part of the politician's image kit.

Those without children are now biting back. They are developing their own equally partisan critique of 'silly', 'self-indulgent' and 'self-righteous' parents. When they are with parents, the childless may repress their desire to talk frankly. But the sense of two mutually incompatible tribes becomes evident when you meet them on their own. At some point in the conversation, there is a moment when, given the freedom to air their pent-up grievances and irritations, each will vent their spleen against the other.

We heard complaints from parents and single mothers about how the arrival of a child meant that their former friends were no longer able to conduct a decent adult relationship with them because of the constant necessity to attend to the trivial demands of their new offspring. We were told about how new mothers were quite irrationally obsessed with their child's abilities, their capacity to read, or sing, or come up with cute observations. We also heard parents blamed for their inability to discipline their children, and unflattering contrasts were frequently drawn between the mother's former 'character' and the way in which she had been diminished or infantilised following the birth of her children.

There appears to be a particular form of scorn reserved for the career woman who has successfully put off childbirth until late in life. It was not the actual decision to try to combine work with child-bearing that attracted the opprobrium – this would have been too ideologically suspect – but the alleged selfishness of the new mother. Sometimes this took the form of work-related complaints about the inconvenience felt by those who had to cover during maternity leave. But sometimes it was more vicious and personal. Such mothers behaved, we were told, 'as though no-one had ever had a baby before', and dark warnings were issued about the likely effects upon the child of such claustrophobic emotional attention. The behaviour of these older mothers was compared unfavourably with 'normal' traditional mothers who, it was said, did not regard childbirth as such a big deal.

Older mothers were thereby placed in a 'no-win' situation. If they attempted to preserve something of their old lifestyle by attending parties and social occasions with child 'in tow' (a popular phrase), they were vulnerable to the charge of wanting to have the best of both worlds; they were, in the currently favoured idiom, 'trying to have it all'. (This phrase has recently become the standard way of reacting to the type of professional working mother depicted in Allison Pearson's novel, *I Don't Know How She Does It.*)

To hear the opinions of some childless people is to understand why separate tribes are developing so rapidly. It would be hard enough for parents if these criticisms were merely general and abstract, but more than once we heard groups of child-free people glorying in specific tales about the most irrational parent and the most loathsome child. Only rarely did anyone feel the need to temper their remarks with some reference to children 'being children' or parents having an impossible job.

Although couples with children were unlikely to hear these criticisms first-hand, we found they often suspected such antagonism. This could produce a highly charged atmosphere. Mothers told us about the tension they sometimes experienced when visited by their childless friends. They found themselves praying that their children would be on their best behaviour and that there would be no disciplinary crises to be overcome. Indeed, some admitted to schooling (or bribing) their children in advance. They also tended to feel that their childless visitors took every opportunity to celebrate their own freedom from responsibilities by producing photographs of, say, their recent trekking holiday in the wilds of Tibet.

In such circumstances it is no great surprise to find that people with children often withdraw from former friends who are childless and instead select new friends who are also parents. This is not merely an adjustment of lifestyle. It suggests that parents and non-parents are now seriously at odds.

It is tempting to turn to psychoanalysis for a plausible explanation of the extreme nature of these opinions. The presence of so much gratuitous hostility between the two tribes suggests that we might be in the presence of a form of reaction-formation, the psychological mechanism that is said to lead those with extreme desires to cope with the impossibility or impracticability of their fulfilment by rounding upon those who have obtained such fulfilment. On hearing the manner in which some childless couples attack the sentimentality of parents and the hatefulness of small children, and comparing it with the way in which those with children mercilessly attack the voluntarily childless for their 'extreme selfishness', it is difficult not to feel that both sides are finding psychological ways to handle desires that their life decisions have made unattainable.

The way in which emotion can drown out reason in this area was clearly demonstrated by the reaction to Sylvia Ann Hewlett's book *Baby Hunger* (entitled *Creating a Life* in America). The book describes the lives and attitudes of successful corporate women in the United States, 40 per cent of whom do not have children. Few of these women, Hewlett found in her in-depth interviews and internet survey, felt that their childless state was either what they wanted or what they had truly chosen.

If the book could be said to have had a target, then it was the men who continue to benefit from an unequal division of domestic labour, and the public authorities and private employers in the US who have done so little to help women reconcile work and parenting. But this is not the impression anyone would have gained from the coverage of the book in newspaper columns, television talkshows and radio phone-ins. In all these media, it was portrayed as either an assault on 'women who want it all', or as an assertion that childless women are unnatural and doomed to a life of regret and remorse. The American parenting experts Darcie Sanders and Martha Bullen spoke for those who had actually read the book when they said: 'We deplore the attempt to stir up controversy by pitting these two populations (mothers and career women) against each other. It is an insult to intelligent women everywhere, whether at home or in the office, to misuse her research as ammunition in the mommy wars.'

Hewlett's book received a huge amount of publicity: the Oprah Winfrey show, the front cover of *Time* magazine and a serialisation in the *Times* of London. But despite this flurry of media attention, sales were well below the publisher's expectations. Commenting on this phenomenon in the *New York Times*, Warren St John concluded, 'Out on the front lines, at the bookstores where publicity turns to sales – or does not – the explanation is all too simple: women are just not interested in shelling out $22 for a load of depressing news about their biological clocks.'

The hostile reaction to *Baby Hunger* – suggests that intolerance of children is now becoming culturally acceptable.In America, Elinor Burkett's book, *Baby Boon: How Family-Friendly America Cheats the Childless*, has provided the impetus for childless people to get together in an organisation called *No Kidding!*. This 'child-free' or 'unburdened' movement (the founders dislike the pejorative connotations of 'childless') now claims to have chapters in 47 American cities and one UK branch in Birmingham. Supporters describe themselves as 'THINKERS' – Two Healthy Incomes, No Kids, Early Retirement – and spend their time either lamenting the tedious conversations they are forced to endure with 'child-burdened' friends, or campaigning for changes in tax and workplace regulations which they insist currently discriminate against those without children.

It would be easier to write off such groups as idiosyncratic if the sentiments they expressed about parents and children found few echoes in popular culture. But as Sylvia Ann Hewlett and Cornell West have shown in *The War Against Parents*, there is good evidence that the media not only sanctions an anti-parent culture but positively celebrates it. Their study of the type of daytime talk-show that dominates the airwaves in most industrialised countries reveals a consistent tendency to present parents as 'either irresponsible fools or in-your-face monsters'. Films like *Home Alone, Honey I Shrunk the Kids, Matilda*, and *Harry Potter* reinforce such attitudes, with their consistent representation of parents as inadequate, uncomprehending, or incompetent. This is not a wholly novel phenomenon but Hewlett and West pointedly contrast this present cultural atmosphere with that which existed in the Fifties, when sit-coms routinely celebrated family togetherness and parental devotion to children. These may appear sexist and sentimental to modern eyes but they at least conceded that parenting was an honourable occupation and that children were sometimes a joy as well as a problem.

Children in today's media representations are rarely joyous. Not only are they seriously underrepresented on television compared to their actual presence in society, but when they do appear in the media they are much more likely to be associated with crime and deviance than with any other form of behaviour. The picture of parents and children and the modern family that emerges from these cultural outputs is as dangerous as it is disturbing. Phil Scraton in *Childhood in Crisis* summarises its components: 'The streets are inhabited by drug users, runaways, joy riders and persistent young offenders. Schools suffer the excess of bullies, truants and disruptive pupils. Families have become "dismembered", replaced by lone mothers, characterised by absent fathers.'

Politicians have not been slow to leap on this particular cultural bandwagon. Parenting classes run by professional social workers are provided to address the inadequacies of amateur mothers and fathers, and antisocial behaviour orders are promoted as the necessary remedy for children who are the products of failed socialisation. It is, as Frank Furedi has argued, a comfortable solution. 'Parents provide an ideal target for those seeking a ready-made one. It is much easier to personalise a moral problem than to understand it as the erosion of an abstract system of values. Immoral people are simpler to recognise than the failure of institutions to transmit meaningful values about the difference between right and wrong. So we pounce on immoral people. And since most immoral people have been brought up by their parents it is tempting to blame their behaviour on their mothers or fathers. After all, if people's behaviour is determined by the action of their parents, whom else should we blame?'

We are not suggesting for a moment that all these sentiments were held by the childless people to whom we talked. But their ready availability within popular culture provides the licence to attack individual mothers and fathers.

It is not our intention to give yet more advice to parents. Parental advice, as we've already observed, is ubiquitous. Nor do we want to add to the litany of complaints about the growing burdens of parenthood. Our aim is to encourage our readers' readiness to participate in what we inelegantly term 'collective reflexivity'. By this we mean our capacity to understand how our lives are shaped by the stories and accounts that are available to us.

The difficulty we have talking coherently and honestly about having and raising kids says a lot about who we are. The next generation of affluent people in the rich world will grow up to unprecedented wealth, knowledge and opportunity. But they must also find a way of living that transcends the character of a time in which the very act of having and rearing children can feel counter-intuitive. To bring up our children to enjoy the best of our times but to avoid the worst has always been the ambition of parents of every generation. It is not an ambition to abandon lightly.

We have not yet mentioned what might be called the most fundamental objection to our original article. This was the irritation felt by some readers at what they saw as the pessimistic tone of our argument. Why, they wondered, did we need to sound so disturbed by the news that women in developed countries are now deciding not to have children or to limit themselves to only one child? If, as we are forever being told, the world is overpopulated, then surely the childless should be celebrated for their unselfish behaviour rather than being subjected to an intensive inquiry into their motives. It might be true that people were not yet thinking along these lines in the places where, arguably, they most needed to – in parts of Africa, for example, where overpopulation could be seen to be having the most disastrous consequences for healthy and happy lives – but at least it was a step in the right direction that might eventually become a universal trend.

Such criticism, however, betrayed a surprising lack of knowledge about the nature and extent of this population decline in developed societies. Many clearly regard it as merely a temporary phenomenon, a demographic hiccup, that will soon be forgotten when the next 'baby boom' comes along. Even those who recognise it as a significant and possibly long-lasting development appear curiously uninterested in the likely social and cultural consequences of such a shift.

We need to determine the precise nature of this 'baby slump' – to understand not only its uniqueness but also the strange way in which it has been largely excluded from political debate. As we will show, it has now become impossible to explain the latest demographic shifts solely in terms of women's demands for gender equality and for careers of their own. They also point to a remarkable change in our views of the value of children.

no babies any more

Matthew. *There's something else that rankles when you start talking in your cavalier way about how children can cramp your style and about how so many of today's parents find child-rearing a terrible drag. You can claim that you were equally unenthusiastic about children 40 years ago. You were a trendsetter. Well done! What you don't take into account is how hard it is for someone like me to take the opposite position. Liking children today can be a lonely business. Most of the people I work with are women. Few of them have children and most of the younger ones simply assume that they don't have to think about kids until they're well into their thirties. Anyone* *who questions such assumptions is not well received. And when the questioner is a man it can attract some real hostility...*

Laurie. *But that's because most women know the score about men and children. They know that even the most conscientious-sounding father is still going to undertake only a tiny share of baby-care and baby-minding. No wonder they gag when they see all those fashion magazine pictures of half-naked male celebrities lifting their newborn child into the air like a football trophy. They know that after the photo-session they'll be the ones who will have to stay behind to change the nappy and wipe up the vomit.*

Matthew. *At least I go home to my own family at the end of the evening and put in some child-minding hours. I may not do as much as Claire would like but there's no way I could get away with being laddish, with saying: 'I'm just off down the pub'. We share the burden.*

***

Even though modern methods of contraception create the opportunity for women to choose whether or not to have children, it is difficult, if not impossible, to know how such choices are actually exercised. There are no doubt some who sit down, with or without a partner, and calculate the pros and cons in a manner that could be described as rational. In less developed countries, people may consciously set out to have as many children as possible, both to increase the family labour force and to mitigate against high rates of infant mortality. But as we have already indicated, in modern Western culture there is considerable resistance to the idea of applying cost-benefit analysis to a decision with such momentous personal and emotional consequences.

Our conversations with parents also revealed a certain antipathy to the very idea of 'choice'. Women spoke about 'finding that they were pregnant' either as the result of an accident or because they or their partner had somehow become casual about contraception. But even this 'casualness' was a complicated business. In some cases it sounded like nothing but carelessness; in others it seemed to be based on a tacit acceptance that if pregnancy occurred as a result of this casualness, then nature should be allowed 'to take its course'.

What, of course, interests us in this book, is not so much the precise manner in which such decisions come to be made as the stories that are likely to be invoked by those who eventually decide to bear children or to remain child-free. We want, in other words, to know the nature of the arguments that allow individuals or couples to feel convinced that they have made the right decision.

The notion that the cultural climate of the time plays a major part in such decision-making was anathema to several readers of our original article. Why, they wondered, were we agonising over the reasons why women choose to have children when the answer was staring us in the face. Women, we were told, had children in response to a biological urge. If a variety of social and cultural factors led them to ignore or repress that urge, then they were denying their fundamental identity. One respondent to our article, James Morton, pithily expressed this line of thought. 'You really can't talk about why women have children without bringing in the reproductive instinct. When I talked about this with my friends they all agreed that instincts were innate and almost impossible to change. No wonder so many women are unhappy when they discover that it is too late to have children. They have flown in the face of their own biological destiny.'

Mr Morton doesn't tell us the gender of the friends with whom he enjoyed such discussion, but it's difficult to believe that they were female. Our own conversations with women always revealed a deep distrust of anything that might be called the 'reproductive instinct'. They were happy to talk about their wish to have children or their sense of fulfilment at having had them, but they understood the cultural objections to the notion that such sentiments were innate.

What sort of instinct is it, after all, that can be so readily ignored by all those women who, with diminishing degrees of guilt and anxiety, choose to remain childless? In the past, if women were sexually active they were likely to become mothers. But as Joan Smith points out, 'the fact that every woman, more or less did, blinded us to the fact that they might not be choosing to do it'. (The *Guardian*, 2 April 2000). Neither do women need to be committed feminists in order to recognise how so-called feminine instincts have in the past provided the dubious basis for arguments about women's proper place being in the home.

None of this means that biology has gone away. Post-feminist advice columns in magazines may shrink from talk of feminine instincts, but the idea that there is something uniquely insistent and overwhelming about a woman's desire to have a child is still current. Here is 'Doctor Tracey' busily comforting one of her readers: 'You're at a time in your life when the urge to have children is so very strong it's hard to keep it under control. And now that you've found Mr Right that makes you want to have a baby even more. I call it "Baby Hunger", and believe me, it doesn't go away, it just gets stronger.'

Most women resist this sort of analysis but some still

fall back upon the idea of a biological clock. For any or all of the reasons that demographers have specified they may not be ready for a child at the moment, but this does not necessarily prevent the growing sense that child-bearing cannot be indefinitely postponed. Reassurance is at hand. In *Help Yourself Cope with your Biological Clock: How to Make the Right Decision about Motherhood*, Theresa Francis-Cheung tells her readers that 'biological clock anxiety is not something to be feared. It is a necessary life-crisis that can help you grow and develop your full potential.' Nothing, she adds, with a nod towards the pre-programmed nature of this anxiety, can stop the clock ticking, but the fact that it is ticking loudly doesn't mean that you have to die childless. 'The really determined woman will find a way, whether it's through fertility treatment or fostering or adoption.' There are specific tips for keeping the pressure at bay. 'Try to limit the amount of time when you think about having a baby to short periods – set aside daily sessions of no more than 20 minutes. When the time is up, stop thinking about it and get on with the rest of your life.'

This type of advice is dangerously optimistic. The widely disseminated notion that one can 'rewind the biological clock' through fertility treatment when the time is right, flies in the face of Sylvia Ann Hewlett's conclusion based on the latest research that a woman in her early forties has, on average, 'a 3-5 per cent shot at achieving a live birth through standard IVF procedures. Not only do women have an extremely hard time getting pregnant at these ages, but a 42 or 44-year-old woman who gets pregnant faces a 50-80 per cent chance of losing her baby through miscarriage.'

There are, of course, other problems with referring to a 'biological clock'. Critics argue that it is yet another devious attempt to suggest that there is something immutable about the reproductive urge. One such critic writes anonymously on a website: 'OK, so where is this biological clock then? If you lie still and I put my ear to your belly, will I hear it ticking? There might indeed be a biological time limit upon women's capacity to reproduce but that is not the same thing as saying that they are genetically predetermined to breed. What we are really talking about here is not an instinct but purely cultural fear and anxiety, the fear of being left behind, the fear of not fitting in with all your friends who have children, the fear of growing old and being lonely, the fear that your partner will leave you if you never have children.'

Even those who are happy to dismiss the idea of the biological clock as nothing more than a convenient device for channelling the multiple dissatisfactions of ageing career women, may find themselves up against a more vigorous opponent when they attempt to wave away the sensations felt by a mother gazing at her new-born child. These nurturing emotions can be so surprising and unexpected that the tendency to reach for an innate explanation becomes almost irresistible.

Those who don't have children receive constant cultural reminders in films and magazines of the desire to nurture that transcends any material or individualistic concerns which might previously have been paramount in their lives. But still it seems difficult to maintain that this urge is exclusively genetic. As Sarah Hrdy (sic) points out in her exhaustive study of the sociobiology of motherhood, *Mother Love: Evolution and the Maternal Instinct*, there is powerful historical evidence that such sentiments are highly contingent. In Paris in 1780, of 21,000 registered births only five per cent were nursed by their mothers. Most of the rest were sent out to the countryside to be wet-nursed by still poorer women. It is interesting to learn that it was men who objected to this practice on the grounds of its unnaturalness. (Hrdy reveals that Linnaeus's chosen name for our class of animals – 'Mammalia' – was related to his own campaign to persuade women to nurse their own children.)

Those who still want to insist upon the existence of a latent maternal instinct will also have to contend with the type of evidence gathered by Ann Oakley in her book, *Becoming a Mother.* Many of the mothers in her sample failed to react at all to this supposedly emotional moment. 'I was completely numbed: I thought I'd be delighted. I think a lot of people won't admit to their feelings. They say they're absolutely delighted, but I'm sure half of them aren't.' Even that figure may be an underestimation. When Oakley asked a group of mothers to describe their feeling 'on first holding the baby', she found that fewer than one in three felt euphoric or proud.

In the end, though, nothing undermines the instinctual thesis more thoroughly than the well-documented evidence that millions of women are now refusing to bear children. It is to the extent and the nature of that refusal that we now turn.

just say no

As our airport bus approached the suburbs of Turin, the courier clicked on her microphone and began to tell us about the beauties of her home-town. In hesitant English she praised its very special chocolates and wonderful piazzas and elegant buildings. She saved her only reservation for the end of her address. 'We used to have a million people in Turin', she said, 'But not now. Now there are only nine hundred thousand. That's the Italians. No babies! No babies any more!'

Some of the British passengers giggled nervously. Why

on earth was the woman getting quite so passionate about procreation in the middle of what was billed in the brochure as a guided tour to the wonders of one of Italy's major cities?

Her outburst would not, though, surprise her fellow Italians. For a long time now they've been digesting the news that a country previously famed for its large happy families is now the home for hundreds of thousands of women who simply refuse to emulate their parents' fertility habits. Large families in Italy are becoming virtually extinct. Many women content themselves with a single child. Many others resolutely decide to remain child-free.

None of these decisions would, of course, have been possible without the efficacy of modern contraceptive techniques. For many years demographers have been busily charting the reductions in national fertility rates which could be expected as a consequence of contraception becoming generally available and culturally acceptable. Even back in the Sixties some experts were expressing concern at the sheer size of the decline. Records at that time showed that the average number of births for each woman in Italy and other industrialised societies had fallen well below the replacement rate of 2.1. (This is the number of children each woman must have to ensure a static overall population). The general consensus, though, was that there was no need to panic. There had been plenty of such downward shifts in previous eras and they had turned out to be little more than temporary trends, statistical blips which soon corrected themselves.

This complacency was misplaced. Today's figures show that fertility rates in many countries have stayed well below the replacement rate. And in some countries the rate has fallen far below even the modest levels recorded in the Sixties. Spain leads the way in Western Europe with a rate of 1.22 per woman, followed closely by Italy with 1.25 and Greece with 1.30.

In the UK, the rate has fallen in nine out of the last ten years and is now standing at 1.64, the lowest since such statistics began to be recorded in 1924, little more than half the fertility rate of 1964, the year of the Baby Boom. One in five women born in that baby boom now reach 40 without themselves having children, a rate of childlessness double that of their mothers' generation. Overall, despite a slight increase in 2000, the fertility rate across Europe is now 1.5.

Fertility decline is now so much an accepted part of the Western European landscape that there was a huge sigh of relief and not a little public rejoicing in France in the early months of 2001 when it was learned that the country now led Western Europe in baby production. Its total of 1.89 babies per woman meant that it had scrambled above the reigning European champion, Ireland, by a massive

0.1. '*Championne d'Europe des bébés*', exulted one newspaper.

Western Europe is not alone. Having children is becoming every bit as unpopular in other parts of the world. More than 60 countries are now recording below or well below replacement rates. Commentators, politicians, and demographers are beginning to express concern about places as diverse as Australia, Singapore, North Korea, Colombia and Bangladesh. Matters are even more serious in Eastern Europe where Latvian and Bulgarian women manage a paltry 1.1 births each, only marginally above the 1.2 currently recorded by the Czech Republic and Estonia.

Those who reject the concerns of the demographers, pointing to the fact that population ageing will mean rising populations in most developed countries for several years to come, should consider the increasingly desperate debate in Japan. The number of Japanese will peak in just four years before beginning an accelerating decline. At current reproduction rates the population will soon be falling by 500,000 per year until 2050 when one in three Japanese will be over 60. If the trend persists until the end of the century, the number of Japanese will have halved. It is hardly surprising that the state and private employers in Japan are offering incentives and rewards to those who reproduce. All have so far failed. Last year

Japan became the first country in history to have more 70-year-olds than ten-year-olds.

There is only marginal comfort to be found in the news that the US and New Zealand are still recording replacement fertility rates. Such rates are almost wholly due to the respective contribution of Hispanic and Maori members of those societies. But even among those groups rates are now showing signs of falling off, another example of the demographic observation that the fertility rates of immigrant and minority groups tend, over time, to conform to the average of the host country.

In the face of such evidence, some demographers are now beginning to think the unthinkable. They are allowing themselves to contemplate a future in which women in the industrial societies of the world might decide to stop having children altogether. What prompts this extraordinary thought is the specific nature of the contemporary decline in fertility rates. Never before in demographic history have they fallen 'so far, so fast, so long, so low, all over the world' (Ben Wattenburg, *The Birth Dearth*).

There is one other notable feature of this decline. In the past it was always possible to point to one or other social or cultural factor, such as an economic boom (or a power strike) which might ensure a reversal of the population trend in the near future. But the reasons confidently cited by demographers for the current slump in fertility are likely to become more rather than less salient in the coming years. It is, for example, generally agreed among experts that there is a strong link between women's decision to remain childless and their eagerness to pursue careers of their own. Survey evidence suggests an acceleration of this process. Women in industrialised societies show no inclination whatsoever to abandon their newfound careers in favour of a return to their traditional housebound role.

Two other factors are found to influence the decision not to procreate: the materialistic imperative not to lower one's standard of living and the cultural imperative to find ways of asserting one's individuality. These tend to be lumped together by moralists as regrettable evidence of a new selfishness, but there is every sign that they are going to become more prevalent. We may object to aspects of consumerism but there is no evidence to suggest that we are developing any resistance to its lure. Nor is there any sign that we are prepared to sacrifice one iota of our hard-won individualism.

No wonder some demographers are throwing up their hands in alarm: the present decline in fertility rates is not only unprecedented; there is no indication on the causal horizon that they might do anything else in the immediate future but fall even further.

Why is it then that Western governments and politicians have been so slow to respond? While declaring it necessary to reduce fertility rates in the Third World, they remain strangely silent about the dramatic population shifts that are occurring within their own territories. In 1999 the United Nations survey of population policies showed that 28 countries with below-replacement-level fertility did admit that their rate was 'too low' but all the English-speaking countries and all the Nordic countries, along with Belgium and the Netherlands, insisted that they were still satisfied with their population levels. After all, despite the falling rates, growing life-expectancy and immigration means that the total population of most developed countries remains roughly stable.

There are other reasons for such relative complacency. Why should governments draw attention to a problem over which they have so little control? Those who have examined the many attempts by democracies to enhance fertility rates through such instruments of social and economic policy as parental leave, tax breaks, cash incentives to have more than one child, and the provision of childcare, have come to one overriding conclusion. None of them appears to work. As the demographer John Ditch observed in his report to the Austrian Institute of Family Studies in 2000: 'No clear relationship can be established between any country's rate of fertility and the form or value of its child support package.'

In fact governments have been unwilling to throw themselves into pro-birth campaigns. The former tennis player and national icon Bjorn Borg was featured on posters urging Swedish people to 'Fuck for Freedom', and in 1997 the Austrian Defence Minister, Werner Fasslabend, announced that women had a patriotic duty to have at least two children. But in general neo-liberal states have been hesitant about interfering in anything so personal as reproductive behaviour. Such an inhibition is probably reinforced by the memories of the 'breeding policies' associated with fascism, and by fear of a feminist backlash against any campaign which appears to suggest, however implicitly, that a women's proper place is in the maternity ward.

There may be even more disturbing reasons for this relative political silence. For, if governments were to embark upon any form of pro-birth campaign, they would be forced to draw attention not only to the falling fertility rate but also to the potential social implications of this phenomenon. They would risk turning generations against each other, with the news that the falling fertility rate will require the shrinking workforce to pay higher and higher taxes in order to meet the cost of looking after the ever-increasing proportion of older people. Interventionist governments would also risk exacerbating the emerging conflict between the two tribes (parents and non-parents) to which we have already alluded.

By far the most dangerous outcome of any government attempt to interfere in reproductive patterns, however, would be an increase in racial tension. Governments could hardly conduct any kind of pro-birth campaign without highlighting the fact that the dramatically falling fertility rate is making it impossible for society to recruit a sufficient number of indigenous workers. They would be forced to explain that this can only be remedied, in the short term at least, by a massive increase in immigration. Racist parties across Europe are already beginning to exploit this. In Germany the anti-immigrant pro-birth line is brutally summarised in the slogan, *Kinder statt Inder*, 'Children instead of Indians', while in Austria, the right-wing populist Jorg Haider is busy playing upon his country's fears that the expansion of the EU to the East will lead to low-paid workers from over the border stealing jobs from the national population.

Those who are intent upon stirring up racist trouble have the statistics to reinforce their case. Demographers such as Peter McDonald of the Australian National University, for example, have already made the telling extrapolations. Consider the case of Italy. If that country is to achieve demographic sustainability (stable population growth) in the future, then it will mean that on average four out of five Italian women will need to have at least one more child. If, as seems much more likely, the fertility rate remains close to its present level of just over one child per woman, then the only way to keep the population constant and available jobs filled will be by increasing the current immigrant numbers from 80,000 a year to 400,000 a year. This is not a once-and-for-all fix. To maintain present population levels, Italy 'would be expected to absorb two million immigrants every five years into the endless future'. Similar calculations have been carried out in Germany by the DIW research institute. These show that by the year 2020 the country will have to import one million immigrants of working age each year simply to maintain the workforce. In Japan, serious consideration is already being given to admitting 500,000 Koreans each year. Politicians there are no doubt vainly hoping that the country's traditional opposition to immigrants will be tempered by the simultaneous promise to send them back home five years later.

Peter McDonald drives the point home with a simple calculation. 'If women, on average, have just one child (and several countries are close to this level) then the size of the generation will halve in one generation which, in demographic terms, is about 28 years. In 56 years, the generation size will be only a quarter of what it was two generations beforehand. In a population with fertility at the current Italian level... the population in the subsequent 100-year period will fall to just 14 per cent of its initial level.'

The idea that this problem can only be solved by hugely increased levels of immigration is a matter of debate. Arguments that developing countries will have to import more workers to fill the gaps left by the ageing population and to generate the wealth to pay for their pensions are rebutted by reference to the eventual ageing of those immigrants. 'Immigrants grow old too. If you import one million people now, then to look after them when they retire, you will need to import 4 million, and then 16 million and so on' (Anthony Browne, *Prospect*, July 2002).

The most overtly political use of population statistics is probably to be found within *The Death of the West* by the former Republican presidential candidate, Patrick Buchanan. After a brisk recitation of the present fertility rates, he feels able to declare that, 'The West is dying. Its nations have ceased to reproduce, and their populations have stopped growing and begun to shrink. Not since the Black Death carried off a third of Europe in the 14th century has there been a graver threat to the survival of Western civilisation... if living standards are not to fall, EU countries may have to allow a 60-fold increase in immigration.'

Some of the most apocalyptic demographic predictions may be fanciful, or politically inspired, and may not allow sufficiently for the capacity of society to adjust to the new demographic circumstances by such measures as raising the retirement age. But political anxiety about the immigration implications of present population trends creates a further barrier to an open and honest debate about the declining rate of reproduction.

For those politicians who have seen the demographic evidence and pondered its implications, there is only one possible justification for their present silence and inactivity – the evidence that women in many Western countries are now delaying the birth of their first child. Figures published in 2001 by the UK Office for National Statistics indicate that the pregnancy rate for women aged 40 and over has risen by more than 40 per cent in the last decade. Over the same period, pregnancy rates for women under 30 fell by nearly 15 per cent. The Netherlands leads the way in late parenthood: the average age of first-time mothers is now nearly 30. Survey evidence also shows that most women who delay having children still have every intention of having at least two 'when the time is right'.

Any optimism engendered by these findings, however, is quickly undermined by other evidence showing that the more women defer reproduction, the more likely they are in practice to opt for only one child or to remain childless. They may also find that they have simply left it too late. It has been estimated that two-thirds of women will be unable to become pregnant spontaneously by the age of 40. Small wonder, perhaps, that nearly one in three of those declaring an intention to have children remain childless five years on, and one in ten, notably the better educated and the richer, announce that they now wish to remain childless. What's more, there are growing signs of this becoming culturally conventional. A recent Mintel survey, cited by Eleanor Mills in a *Spectator* article provocatively headlined 'Too Busy To Have Babies', found that one in four women didn't wish to have children because they did not want to give up their careers. Mills quotes 30-year-old Beth, a television news producer: 'I've put in the hard work and I'm finally at the stage where my job is fun. I love it. Why should I give up everything I've worked for? I couldn't possibly do this job with a kid and I wouldn't want to.' But wasn't that rather a selfish attitude? Mills enquired. The response was instant. 'It's much more selfish to bring more children into an over-populated world'. (There is now an acronym for women like Beth: 'SARAH' – Single, Rich And Happy.)

One way in which women like Beth can avoid any of the residual stigma that is attached to the childless without jeopardising their careers, of course, is to opt for a single child. But we must recognise that even this modest numerical compromise represents a dramatic change in our attitudes to children. In the past the single child was rarely a chosen option. Only children were popularly regarded as something of a freak, a genetic aberration. At the turn of the 20th century, the much respected childcare expert, G. Stanley Hall, conducted a massive study of only children and came to the firm conclusion that they were 'peculiar and exceptional'. Large families, he insisted, were necessary to successful rearing. It was obvious really.

One only had to look to nature for confirmation. 'It will be noticed that all creatures which have large families... have less trouble in rearing them than those which have only one or two young. Little pigs are weeks ahead of young calves, and the young partridge, with its dozens of brothers and sisters, is far more teachable than the young eagle.' Being an only child, asserted Hall, 'was a disease in itself'.

We might not now assent to the idea of the single child as 'diseased', but until very recently there was still plenty of lay and expert opinion confirming the view that only children were much more likely to be self-centred, spoilt, attention-seeking, dependent and temperamental. No wonder, then, that so much publicity has been accorded to research by Toni Falbo of the University of Texas which provides welcome empirical reassurance to parents who choose to limit their family in this way – though it represents quite a shift in thinking. When she started studying 'singletons' in the Seventies, Falbo, herself an only child with one child of her own, found that professional journals and lay magazines were falling over themselves to publicise her research evidence about the normality of only children. It was, she writes, 'believed that only children were a disaster. But you can't get that attention any more. The general view is that, by and large, they are ordinary folk.' Her own extensive research conducted in the US and in China – where there has been much talk about the negative consequences of the strict 'one child policy' – found that only children scored significantly better in 'achievement motivation and personal adjustment' but were in all other respects indistinguishable from children with siblings.

It was as well that Falbo came up with such positive evidence because mothers had already voted on the issue with their bodies. Only 20 years ago the most popular reason given by parents for having a second child was the desire to prevent their first-born being an 'only'. But, as we have seen, such concerns no longer seem to hold. In 1998, nearly one in five 50-year-old women in the US had given birth to only one child, close to double the number of two decades earlier, a massive 85 per cent increase since

1980. In the US now, one in five of all children are single-tons. In Portugal the figure rises to one in three.

Much of this demographic analysis is informed by the pernicious assumption that the decline in the birth rate can be entirely attributed to choices made by women. Look at the facts, say the experts. Fertility only declines significantly in those countries where women have access to their own contraceptive techniques. *Ergo* – women must be the 'guilty party'. This simple conclusion then provides moralisers with a splendid opportunity to demonise women for 'selfishly' rejecting the emotional satisfactions of motherhood in favour of the material advantages provided by a job and career.

But matters are much more complex. In modern mid-dle-class relationships, decisions about whether or not to have children are increasingly the result of a discussion between partners and there is no evidence whatsoever that the men involved in such debates are any more pre-disposed to favour procreation than women. Indeed, many of the women we spoke to who had delayed child-birth or had only one child said that their boyfriends or husbands played a big part in their decision. Many older women who had decided not to have children told us that their decision had been strongly influenced by their male partner's desire not to lose the benefits they enjoyed from having a dual income. There is also evidence that women who marry divorced men are much more likely to restrict themselves to one child because their new partner already has children from a previous relationship and makes it clear that he wants no more.

Indeed it seems the more men are required to think about, adjust to, and make sacrifices for their children the more they become a driver of declining fertility. The news that high-flying American men have many more children than similarly successful women is attributed by Sylvia Ann Hewlett to the capacity of rich men to find young wives willing to stay at home and organise the nanny in exchange for the financial security of their husband's income. Men on more modest incomes are likely to think twice about having children if they know they will be expected to make more personal sacrifices. But any such sacrifices will still be modest. Women in relationships who are contemplating bringing a child into the world have to cope not only with the knowledge that they are almost certainly going to assume the major responsibility for that child's nurturing, but also with the statistical evidence which shows that the father is likely to leave home well before the child reaches adolescence. In half of all the existing family units in major Western cities, the father has virtually disappeared. In nearly all such cases, the children have remained with the mother. (The relatively few instances in which this outcome is the result of a contested divorce are hardly enough to affect the general picture.) Full-time fatherhood is now a short-lived career – a career quickly terminated at the lower end of the social scale by desertion and at the upper end by divorce.

Even when fathers do stay around there may be other unfortunate consequences for the mothers of their children. In those Southern European countries where childbirth out of wedlock is still stigmatised, part of the reason why women choose not to procreate is because to do so means getting married to men who continue to expect a traditional household division of labour and authority. In other words, Italian and Spanish women have not turned against children but against the failure of men to adjust to women's expectations of equality and freedom. Conversely, the reason why birth rates may have held up better in northern European countries is that both social attitudes and welfare provision mean women can choose to become mothers without having to become wives.

When all these elements (and prospects) are taken into account, it becomes easy to see why a woman's decision not to have children is as readily (or more readily) explained by her fears about future paternal conduct as by her own 'selfishness'. It also helps to explain why more and more women are deciding that life might be simpler if they choose to dispense with 'father' altogether and go it alone.

As we said at the beginning of this chapter, neither of us ever actually decided to have children. Maybe this was in part because we saw this as a woman's choice and a woman's responsibility. One sobering reflection is that the more having children becomes a man's choice and a man's responsibility the fewer men seem willing to say 'yes'. Paradoxically, this means there is both a progressive and a traditionalist policy response to declining fertility. Progressives can convincingly argue that we need to make it easier for women to have children outside marriage; while traditionalists can argue that men will only want more children if they can expect women to take on most of the work and sacrifice involved. That neither of these policy responses seems credible highlights again the strength of the forces driving down fertility rates.

There is of course another option – that men change. There is no question that this would mean men had to accept more responsibility and make more sacrifices. But for men to undertake such a transformation, they really need to know why they want to be fathers in the first place. What they need is a strong account of the virtues of fatherhood. And, unless they get it, they will continue by their behaviour and their attitudes to be key drivers of the baby slump.

We have no wish to be apocalyptic about the present trends in fertility. Of course the current rate of decline cannot persist forever. Take this simple extrapolation – without any changes in the present rates, and without recourse to massive immigration, the population of the European Union will shrink from its present 375 million to 75 million by 2200. By the time we reach the next millennium there will only be 50,000 people left in Europe to join in the celebrations!

This conclusion is patently absurd. But it hardly invalidates the present evidence of a population crisis. When serious contemporary students of population, using considerably more sophisticated techniques than their predecessors, are forced to admit that they cannot see any indication of a reversal of these trends in the near future, then it is surely time to ask why it is that women and men, in such huge and increasing numbers, are so resolutely opting for childlessness.

Demographers, as we have shown, fully expected the general availability of contraception to affect fertility rates: they recognised the manner in which it would enable women to plan their lives, to decide the best way to make child-bearing compatible with their careers and desire for self-expression. What they had not expected, though, was that women in many cases might use this new control over fertility in order to stop having children altogether or to confine themselves to a single child. This is the sort of previously 'unthinkable' development that can only be fully understood by a shift in our sense of the value of children – our increasing uncertainty about how they might contribute to our own sense of well-being. What must now concern us, therefore, are the possible reasons for this loss of faith in children.

costs and risks

Laurie. *I genuinely wish you didn't have to talk so much about your 'burden', that you got more joy or pleasure out of being a father. That's why your story doesn't add up. Half the time you're presenting yourself as the emotionally rounded modern man and the other half you're complaining about how terribly hard it is to manage. For the last eight years there's been one uniform feature of our get-togethers. Whenever I ask 'How are you?', I can be sure that I'm going to get a lengthy catalogue of your problems studded with phrases like 'knackered' and 'stressed out'.*

Matthew. *Maybe I wouldn't be so tired or talk about it so much if you weren't so obviously enjoying your freedom from responsibilities of any kind. Tell you what. Give up your ageing playboy lifestyle, buy a nice granddad cottage in the country with a big garden and a golden Labrador and then have the kids over for a long weekend. I guarantee that you'd then get a very different script from me.*

Laurie. *I'm not sure that you'd let them come to me even if I did all that. When you were Joe's age you used to play out in the street from the end of school till bedtime. When you fell in the canal I only found out because you came home with wet clothes. On holidays, you were largely expected to entertain yourself. But you won't so much as let your own kids run down to the corner shop on their own. You practically never let the children out of your sight. You constantly feel that you have to entertain them even if that means buying into every overhyped craze the media throws at you. What did you say when I asked you how you'd enjoyed your holiday in Italy? 'Great but exhausting'.*

***

There were a number of occasions when our friends and

colleagues became noticeably bored by our lengthy sociological attempts to explain why fertility rates were falling at such a dramatic pace in so many European countries. They began to nod wearily as we described women's unreadiness to abandon their new-found careers for the supposed joys of motherhood and the difficulties that both men and women found in reconciling their desire for self-development with the sacrifices required by parenting.

It was usually at moments like this that someone in the room declared that we were making a mountain out of a molehill, that the real reason why people were choosing not to procreate had little to do with sociology. It came down to plain old economics. Anyone with a pencil and paper could work it out for themselves. Children had become too expensive. They cost too much. Hadn't we ever done the actual sums?

This was precisely the development in attitudes to child-bearing that was envisaged more than half a century ago by the political and economic theorist, Joseph Schumpeter in *Capitalism, Socialism and Democracy*. Schumpeter had no time for the Marxist argument that the bourgeoisie would eventually be ousted by the revolutionary working class. He envisaged that their disappearance would be effected more peacefully but no less successfully by modern economics.

'As soon as men and women learn the utilitarian lesson... as soon as they introduce into their private lives a sort of inarticulate system of cost accounting – they cannot fail to become aware of the heavy personal sacrifices that family ties and especially parenthood entail under modern conditions and the fact that at the same time, excepting in the case of farmers and peasants, children cease to be economic assets.'

We do not have to look far to find support for Schumpeter's thesis. Although few people ever admitted to us that they had used an explicit system of cost accounting before deciding whether to procreate, there is no shortage in our culture of references to the cost of having children. In the first two months of 2002 alone, we came across four different surveys or calculations in national UK newspapers and magazines which provided just such a checklist for prospective parents.

These accounts were clearly in tune with the views of many of our interviewees. Over and over again we were told that children cost more in cash terms than ever before. We were told stories about the price of nappies, baby food and toddler clothes. Without any prompting, our interviewees recalled how much they had spent on birthday and Christmas presents for their children, We became used to learning that 'kids, today, cost a bomb'.

At first we took these stories at face value, but their

ubiquity eventually forced us to examine the claims they contained in more detail.

Estimating what might be called 'the running costs' of children is far from easy. One authoritative UK study suggests an average figure of £3,000 per year, while an American estimate prepared by the US Government in 2000 (as part of an educational programme aimed at encouraging teenagers to wait until they are more financially secure before having children) suggested that a middle-income family would spend about $146,780 to raise a child to 18.

But there really is no such thing as an average family or average child. As we found from a couple of exchanged glances and awkward pauses in our conversations, some parents view as an absolute necessity what others see as a luxury. These differences are not just about the treats we buy our children. A recent survey of middle-class mothers in one newspaper managed to find a range of annual spending on nappies starting at £300 and peaking with a Mrs Phaedra Applin who claimed to have spent £1,300 on nappies for her son Aston (*Daily Mail* 16.3.01). (Ms Applin's budget also included £5 per week for 'baby massage'.)

A rather more up-market survey by the *London Magazine* added in the costs of private school and part-time nannies and came up with a 'total cost' from birth to 21 of £317, 857. In case its readers hadn't realised the opportunity costs involved in such expenditure, the magazine helpfully added a list of alternative ways of spending the money, including:

Buy a pair of brand-new matching his and hers Silver Seraph Rolls Royce's... Purchase a Princess 50 motor yacht, complete with two staterooms and twin berth guest cabin... Become the proud owner of an original Damien Hirst spot painting.

Of course, how much parents spend depends on their income, and how they choose to define their children's needs. Parents of child prodigies in sports or music consider a fortune spent on equipment and training as essential expenditure, as do those parents who impoverish themselves by their efforts to cater for offspring with special educational or emotional needs.

There is also the problem of timescale. Those without children often explained their current disinclination to procreate by reference to the increasing number of years that modern children 'stayed around'. New mothers might be blissfully content and lovey-dovey buying pretty clothes and special treats for their cute little babies, but they might not be so happy when it begins to dawn on them that this is a project (and an expense) that is going to last a lifetime. Children nowadays are less ready to leave home and proceed to make their own way in the world. Many are still likely to be living and consuming at home until their early twenties, and even more will be relying upon their parents to provide substantial funds towards the ever-increasing costs of their higher education. 'You never get rid of them these days,' we were told.

But it wasn't just the simple 'running' costs that dominated cost-benefit discussions of children, it was the perils of child-focused consumerism. Parents and non-parents were united in their recognition of a whole set of 'secondary needs' that were not generated by the child's intrinsic requirements but by the external marketplace. Suddenly such previously unknown goods as Pokemon cards, Harry Potter and Spiderman T-shirts had become essential requirements for every properly accoutred small child. Discreet toys like the hula-hoop and the spinning top had given way to products like the Playstation that required continuous injections of more capital: £40 for each new game, or £3.50 a night to hire one from the video store. A marketplace of branded goods that had previously only become relevant during early adolescence had now successfully extended itself backward through the years until it reached the romper suit. A recent survey by the consumer research company, Mintel, found that body sprays were now used by nearly three out of every four nine-ten-year-old girls, while hair gel was used by the same proportion of boys who found it 'essential for their trendy hairstyles'. Eight out of ten girls and seven out of ten boys now choose their own clothes. Brands like Nike and Adidas and chains like Gap Kids stalk the world with their high value-added pitch for parental purchases. Even neonates are now fair game. A recent Gap advertisement shows a pregnant woman and the slogan, 'For All Generations'.

There's one obvious piece of advice that can be offered to parents overwhelmed by the scale and cost of this kiddie cornucopia (listen carefully and you might hear it whispered by grandparents). They can always say 'no'. But one of the explicit aims of child- and parent-focused marketing is to make saying 'no' harder. According to the website *Globalissues*, two billion dollars is spent annually on advertising to young consumers in America alone. The way marketing has muscled in on the parent child relationship has been well captured by Dan Cook in 'Lunchbox Hegemony, Kids and the Marketplace':

> Observe a child and parent in a store. That high-pitched whining you'll hear coming from the cereal aisle is more than just the pleading of single kid bent on getting a box of Fruit Loops on to the shopping cart. It is the sound of thousands of hours of market research, of an immense co-ordi-

nation of people, ideas and resources, of decades of social and economic change all rolled into a single, 'mommy, pleeease!'

When so many resources are devoted to the children's market, it is hardly surprising to hear parents lament that they have little alternative but to ride along with the latest craze. They certainly get no help from government. Despite all the evidence about how the market researchers are able to stimulate small children's desires, there is little effective regulation in this area. Only in Sweden, where family policy is an active force rather than a political add-on, can one find a proper counterattack. The response in that country to the news that children under ten were incapable of telling the difference between a TV advertisement and a programme, and could not understand the purpose of an advertisement until the age of 12, was swift and effective. Since 1992, Sweden has banned all advertising during children's prime-time television.

Suggestions that similar measures be adopted elsewhere are frequently regarded as some sort of interference with the sovereignty of market forces or as disturbing evidence of the advance of the nanny state. Commentators who are only too eager to protect the 'innocence' of children from the risks posed by speeding cars and roaming paedophiles remain remarkably sanguine in the face of the news that those same innocent children are being taught what to value by people with no other moral agenda other than the bottom line. The objects at issue in this debate may seem banal enough – the latest pair of trainers, the most recent version of a favourite football shirt – but the cost of these objects becoming objects of desire for very young children can be monumental.

Again and again we are confronted with lurid tales of the exorbitant costs of Christmas and the horrors of chasing from shop to shop in a desperate search for that year's must-have toy. In 1997, in research for the Joseph Rowntree Foundation, Middleton, Ashworth and Braithwaite found that children receive presents to an average value of £250 at Christmas (the word 'value' here is of course a reference to cost, not to the intrinsic worth of the mountains of overpriced junk foisted on desperate parents).

Christmas is supposed to be the happiest time of year for families but for many it has become more like an assault course: 'Christmas has become an annual financial nightmare. Poorer parents often resort to catalogue shopping or taking out high interest loans.' (Middleton et al.)

However, the same research offered evidence that our own overwhelmingly middle-class social circle found less easy to accept: 'Some parents are, apparently, determined to resist the financial pressures of Christmas. Parents in professional/managerial families spend less at Christmas on babies and pre-school children than in any other socio-economic group.' (Middleton et al.)

This finding is not limited to Christmas. Other research shows quite clearly that well-off people spend a much lower proportion of income on their children than the poor do. Indeed, well-off parents, who earn two or three times more than their poorer fellow citizens, only spend around a fifth more on their children.

The more we examined this type of evidence, the more we began to believe that the middle-class parents and non-parents to whom we spoke were using 'costs' as a form of rationalisation, a way of avoiding discussion about other more troubling matters associated with having children. We say this because, at the risk of sounding like Scrooge before the ghosts, there is little question that the absolutely essential costs of child-rearing, such as food, heating, and clothes have fallen in comparative terms. And many of the other essentials are universally provided – however inadequately – by the welfare state.

Which brings us on to another factor that tends to inflame the debate between parents and the child-free. Often overlooked in discussions about the costs of children is spending on public services. Children (and thus their parents) are the beneficiaries of most education spending, and in healthcare and welfare spending are second in the queue behind elderly people.

For most parents this is as it should be. It is, they think, only appropriate that the state recognises the sacrifices that rearing children routinely demands. But state subsidies for parents were not, we found, so popular with childless adults. This tribe argued that those who had children should take responsibility for their upbringing themselves; they could not see why they should pay taxes to support those who were merely adding to the problems of an overcrowded world.

This is a debate that looks like hardening over the coming years. As governments are forced to face the type of population issues that we outlined in the last chapter, issues about fertility and childcare are bound to rise to the top of the agenda. One important consequence of this may be a change in the politics of tax and spend. Instead of the familiar debate about the gap between the rich and poor, and the equally familiar dispute between the egalitarian left and the free market right, we may be seeing the beginnings of a battle between those with children and those without. Parents, ever more resentful of what they see as the rising burdens of childcare, will start arguing more vigorously for stronger public services, while the growing army of the childless will increasingly declare their resentment at paying taxes that they regard as little more than family subsidies.

Whenever we challenged middle-class parents' assertions about the costs of children by pointing to the relatively small proportion of their income that they devoted to them (compared to the poor) or to the relatively disproportionate claims they were able to make on public services (compared to the child-free), we were confronted with one other critical cost. Women who are endeavouring to have children and maintain a career have to face the extra cost (and anxiety) of finding adequate childcare for children during the early years. They might also face further financial penalties because of the manner in which their status as a mother diminishes their promotion prospects. Taking time off for maternity leave or because of a child's sickness can often seriously affect career development, despite bland managerial assurances to the contrary.

This is a significant concern. The increase in women's employment is the single most marked trend in the labour market over recent decades. Following this trend, although moving more slowly, has been an increase in women's earnings potential. The equation looks straightforward. As more women choose to work and as those women improve their salaries, so the opportunity costs of mothers' absence from the labour market increases.

According to the UK Government's Women's Unit in 1999, young single women without children took home on average £252 a week, whereas single women in the same age group with children received only £128 a week. When other elements, such as lost opportunities for training and pension contributions, are taken into account, one UK estimate puts the potential net income cost of having children for women at over a quarter of a million pounds. If the total opportunity costs – examining what women could have earned over their life without any interruptions – are taken into account, then the final figure comes out at anywhere between £100k and £1 million (Kathrine Rake, 'Women's Income Over the Lifetime', *The Stationery Office*, 2000).

Echoing this work in America, Anne Crittenden has claimed: 'This forgone income, the equivalent of a huge "mommy tax", is typically more than $1 million for a college educated woman.' (*The Price of Motherhood*, 2001)

The fact is that in our competitive, long hours, work culture, parents are at a disadvantage. The image of the hassled mother or father late from the school run turning up at work with clothes plastered in peanut butter or baby goo is a situation comedy staple. Parents are less free to work late and less free to travel as part of their job or to take a better job. They are more likely to have to take time off due to family illness or a breakdown in child-care.

Small wonder that when one asks any new parent about the biggest change they've noticed in themselves since the birth of their child, they will invariably say, as they smother a yawn, 'sheer bloody exhaustion'. Liberal employers may make some attempts to help employees reconcile the demands of home and work, but there is little evidence that they are having much impact on the general picture. The UK Women's Unit stated in February 2001 that '83 per cent of women believe that commitment to family responsibilities hinders women's advancement in the workplace'.

Many of the child-free colleagues of these working parents clearly feel that it serves them right if they suffer from split loyalties. Following the UK government's decision in 2001 to require employers to give serious consideration to parental requests for more family-friendly working patterns, AOL carried out a poll amongst its Internet subscribers. How would they choose to describe the new policy initiative? Was it 'a good decision for families' or did it mean 'more burdens on business'. A distinct majority opted for a third alternative. They declared that the new policy was 'unfair to other employees'.

In November 2001 a typical exchange took place in the pages of two UK Sunday newspapers. In the course of predicting the emergence of an anti-parent backlash in the UK like that already evident in the US, Tessa Boase in the *Sunday Times* described the routine exploitation of the childless by mothers and fathers:

> Another childless woman complains of a new executive mother who would arrive at the office, put her feet up on the desk every day and exclaim: 'It's so lovely to be able to read the papers over a cappuccino.' Yet another complains of a mother who spent all day looking for a pair of Baby Spice satin pyjamas on the Internet lest her daughter have a tantrum. None of these child-free women wishes to identify herself because it is politically incorrect to criticise parents – especially those doing the supermum juggling act. Because parenting is now presented as an achievement rather than an inevitable milestone (one mummy newspaper column actually calls itself 'How DOES she do it?'), the childless don't dare to criticise because they have No Idea How Difficult It Is.

Jeannette Hyde in the *Observer* raced to the defence of working mothers:

> If you looked into the matter, you'd probably find that the mothers among your colleagues are doing mountains of work you never see. Replying to work e-mails by remote access at the weekend, fitting in paperwork when children have an afternoon nap, or doing budget reports on the lap-

top at eight after the kids go to bed. It is as if society and the media have said: these women are fair game. They abandon their kids by putting their own interests first, therefore they must take the stick. If you can't take the heat, get back in the kitchen.

This battle has another front. Parents, busily defending themselves from those like Elinor Burkett, who attack their 'special privileges' at work, are also liable to find themselves assailed by those who argue that however hard parents (or more usually, mothers) try to balance work and home they always end up damaging the child.

Maria Scott (also in the *Observer*) briskly captures this particular dilemma:

> Damned if you do, damned if you don't: if you stay at home to look after your children, you are likely to feel patronised by those who are working, even your partner. You also lose your financial independence. If you actually want to return to work but are staying at home because you think this is best for your children, you may end up resenting them. And if you return to work, you are likely to feel guilty over just about everything.

Scott vividly captures the dilemmas facing the modern working mother, yet however hard and however costly it is for today's mother to reconcile family and home, their position is surely better than that of their mothers who had an absolute choice between career and family.

Over and again in our discussions we came across this predicament. Parents, and particularly mothers, felt that they were faced either with unreal choices or choices between two equally unpalatable alternatives. But once or twice another theme emerged, which unexpectedly united the two tribes. Mothers who'd talked about the extreme difficulties of combining work and children and women who had 'decided' to remain childless in order to pursue their careers began tentatively to admit that perhaps they were underplaying their love of the sense of independence and individualism provided by work.

It is not difficult to understand this tentativeness. Independence and individualism are typically regarded as admirable traits in our society (even if extreme forms like 'narcissism' may be declared pathological). But the problem is that when such terms are used by parents and non-parents in the context of a discussion about the value of children, they have an unfortunate tendency to elide into the distinctly pejorative trait of 'selfishness'.

It is, for example, increasingly acceptable for someone to leave the parental home or abandon a partner in the name of individualism and independence but not for a career woman to cite these goals as an explanation of her childlessness or for a mother to use them to explain why she continues to work, even when she does not actually need the money and knows that she is possibly harming her children in the process.

The charge often made by critics of working mothers is that 'they want it all'. In an important sense this is true, as is the much less frequently expressed charge that, 'Fathers have always had it all and don't intend to give any of it up to make things easier for the women.' And, in the end, this was the hard conclusion to which our discussions led us. We understood how sincere our friends were when they talked about the costs and sacrifices of having children but, however much they made their case, there simply wasn't the objective evidence to back them up. This returned us to our original and more sociological intuition. What explains the gap between the reality of declining real costs and increasing opportunities for parents and the perception of growing burdens and choices denied, lies in a very different, less tangible and less easily articulated, sense of sacrifice – the loss of those modern absolute values: autonomy and freedom and individualism.

When we persuaded a few of our friends to abandon, or at least temporarily suspend, their emphasis upon the role of cost in their choices about child-rearing, we were surprised by the amount of anguish that began to surface.

Sylvia Ann Hewlett's career women may have felt profoundly sad about the sacrifices that their career 'choices' had imposed upon them, but there was also sadness among our own sample of mothers (and fathers) who were often vainly trying to reconcile their decision to have children with their determination to go on finding personal occupational fulfilment.

Schumpeter predicted correctly that as we became freer to choose how to live our lives and spend our money we would be more inclined to let the question of whether or not we have children become a matter of self-conscious choosing. What he did not predict was how miserable so many people would become as a result of this extended rationalism.

***

There was another and quite different dimension which often arose when the conversation turned to the costs of family life – that having children is now a much more risky business than it was in previous times because of the increasingly dangerous nature of the environment in which they must be reared. Many of our discussions took place around the time of the abduction and murder of the British school girl Sarah Payne and the subsequent campaign for a 'Sarah's law', based on 'Megan's law' in

America, which would reveal to parents the whereabouts of convicted paedophiles. It seemed every parent had a hair-raising story of losing their child in a department store, on a beach or at a fairground, and of the possible dangers that might have resulted. The fear of 'stranger danger' is steadily rising amongst parents. It now constitutes the main reason offered by parents for driving their children to school.

We also became accustomed to learning about the new health 'risks' that were currently facing children. The controversy over the MMR vaccine was in full flight at the time of our conversations and many parents of young children were agonising over whether or not to vaccinate – a decision which, on the one hand, might mean their own children infecting others with measles and mumps and, on the other, might lead to their own child becoming autistic. Other threats to life and sanity loomed on the horizon. Many parents had kitchen cupboards that spoke of their intermittent attempt to hold back the tide of pesticides, E-numbers or infected prions that according to 'well-informed reports' and 'scientific tests' might threaten their child's well-being. The 'evidence' of the harm that parents could inadvertently cause their children was also documented in bulging shelves of books advising them on how they should reconnoitre each stage of their child's development, and warning of the consequences that might befall any child whose parent failed to follow the advice. Although all these experts claimed that their aim was to support parents, the overwhelming impression we gained was that its main effect was to create feelings of guilt and inadequacy.

The growth in parental anxiety prompted by such texts and by the ubiquity of 'child care experts' in newspapers and on television has been brilliantly charted by Frank Furedi in his book *Paranoid Parenting*. As he points out, our growing fear of the risks that lie in wait for children, whether concealed in supermarket food, or hidden behind the bushes in the local park, stands in marked contrast to the evidence that children in the affluent nations are now safer, less at risk of premature death and more likely to grow into healthy adults than at any time in history. Although the figures are so low as to make meaningful comparison difficult, it even seems the risk of 'stranger danger' is in decline.

There is another ubiquitous fiction about having children: that parents have less and less time to spend with their offspring. Once again, the evidence points the other way. A study of nearly a thousand parents in late 2001 by the UK-based Future Foundation found that parents now spend around three times as long with their children (90 minutes per day) as they did 40 years ago. This confirms evidence collected by the sociologist Jonathan Gershuny (cited by Furedi) that in 1995 full-time employed women spent more time with their children than non-employed women did in 1961. (The reasons for this may be closely linked to the fact that children are allowed out to play on their own much less than in the past). The cumulative effect of all such views is the creation of a deficit model of parenting.

There is, however, one area of risk that does appear to have grown – the possibility that your child will grow up depressed, neurotic and/or with a dangerous addiction to alcohol or drugs. Indeed there is a powerful body of evidence to suggest that today's youngsters – despite their privileges and opportunities – are more disturbed or mal-adjusted than their parents. This is the subject for another book. But there can be no doubt that today's chil-dren are exposed earlier and more often to drugs, crime and casual sex than they were in previous generations. At a time when a majority of 15-year-olds living in cities will have had sex, taken a variety of drugs, and been physi-cally attacked, it is only reasonable for parents to com-plain that their own attempts to bring up their children are constantly subverted by the street-level realities of youth culture.

There is, though, another consideration that is highly relevant to the present discussion. Some of the causes of present 'maladjustment' or 'distress' among adolescents might well lie within the family. The risk of having a child who is unable to resist the lure of drugs, crime or relentless promiscuity is not wholly external. It is at least arguable that such reliance upon street culture could be the result of being raised in families where the very reason for their existence is ambiguous or uncertain. Many a rebelling or depressed teenager has challenged their parents with such apparently melodramatic questions as, 'Why was I born?' or, 'Why did you have me in the first place?'. One can only wonder at the effect upon them of realising that their parents are singularly unable to provide a proper or plausible answer.

lost inheritances

Matthew. *I remember you coming to my secondary school when I was about 15. It was pretty unusual for you to show up on such an occasion. By then you'd almost completely abdicated all responsibility for my welfare to Jennie. But at least you were there and that was enough to encourage me to ask you about my future. I told you that I was fed up at school and fancied dropping out for a year or two and then taking my A-levels at a further education college and then going on to university. And what did you say? You said that it was entirely up to me. The same old hippie cop-out.*

Laurie. *But what was so wrong about leaving it up to*

you? My parents may have nagged me incessantly about the need to get a good degree and a good career but you'd already made it. You were middle class already. You'd had a good education. You could choose your own future. I'd like to know what you're going to do differently with your own children. Have you got their careers mapped out?

Matthew. *No, I haven't. But that's not because I've abdicated responsibility like you did. It's because the world has changed. I'll hardly need to spend hours telling Joe and Cornell about the intellectual, social and economic advantages of higher education when going to university has become almost a routine destination for middle-class kids like them. And neither can I push them towards specific careers when careers hardly exist any more. I wish it were otherwise.*

***

It was obvious that James was pleased with his present lecturing job. He told us that he had always wanted to be a chemist and nothing gave him greater pleasure than sharing his enthusiasm with university undergraduates. His father had been a chemical engineer and had always gone out of his way to interest his young son in the subject by taking him on long trips round the laboratories where he spent much of his working life, and plying him with larger and larger chemistry sets. James still remembered the day when his father had brought a lump of sodium home from work to conduct a little experiment and managed to set fire to the wardrobe in the back bedroom.

We were holding a conversation with a small group of friends about the extent to which it was now possible for parents (and particularly fathers) to take a real pride in the achievements of their own children. One or two people round the table talked about feeling proud of their offsprings' relative success at school and college and their subsequently going to university, but James doubted if one could take much genuine pleasure from such general educational success. 'We're all middle class, aren't we? It would be pretty odd if our kids hadn't got a few A-levels and a place at university. I don't think we can take much credit for that.' It was when he was pushed to say what would make him proud of his own children that he reverted to his love of chemistry. 'I'd love it if a child of mine thought the same way that I do about chemistry. If he was as interested in the subject as I am and as my dad was. There are some tremendously exciting things happening in the subject at the moment and it would be nice to have a child who would go on to understand more than I ever did. That would be great.'

He looked slightly shamefaced after he'd made his little speech and it wasn't difficult to understand the reasons for his embarrassment. Nowadays there's a reluctance to formulate such specific trajectories for our children. We know that the chances of them following the same job or vocation as ourselves are extremely slim.

In the first half of the twentieth century, there was a common assumption that sons would take up their fathers' occupation and that women would assume a housekeeping role. This was almost as true at the top of the social order as at the bottom. Sons dutifully followed their fathers into the cottage industries, the cotton mills and the coalmines with the same regularity and sense of inevitability that they followed them into the law, the church, or the army. (Even the most marginal professions could be transmitted. In the early Seventies, the official UK executioner, Albert Pierrepoint, wrote about the pride he'd felt in being able to carry on the same profession as his father and grandfather.) Those, like the poet John Betjeman, who decided not to follow their father's occupation could be assailed by guilt throughout their life: they were, somehow, denying their proper destiny. Their fathers had been dishonoured:

In later years,
Now old and ill, he asked me once again

To carry on the firm, I still refused
And now when I behold, fresh-published, new
A further volume of my verse, I see
His kind grey eyes look woundedly at mine
I see his workmen seeking other jobs,
And that red granite obelisk that marks
The family grave in Highgate Cemetery
Points an accusing finger at the sky

(Summoned by Bells, 1960)

What effect does the disappearance of this type of patrimonial expectation have upon people's current views of the meaning of children? Our enquiries revealed that parents, and particularly fathers, were not so much worried about their child's eventual occupation as about their own lack of transmittable skills or trade secrets. The jobs in the 'new economy' that have replaced traditional 'inherited' occupations may attract status and high salaries, but is it really possible for a management consultant or an advertising executive or an investment analyst to think of their position as a family profession with clear-cut skills and a distinctive culture that might be bequeathed to their children? The image of a management consultant leading his young son into the atrium of KPMG plc and announcing, 'One day, son, all this will be yours,' is hardly compelling.

In the past, one of the other great pleasures of having children lay in the confident expectation that they would be inheritors of one's moral code or ideology. Devout Christians and committed socialists and even thorough-going libertarians were confidently able to regard their children as the next generation of apostles for the cause in which they believed. (One Sixties Californian father who had been heavily involved in the idealistic student move-ment of that period told us that he'd regarded his own children as people 'who would finish off the job' that he and his peers had begun.)

We've now become so sceptical about the possibility of our children turning out to be apostles of our ideals that we've forgotten the moral imperative that once informed this prospect. Advice to one's children, whether pompously delivered by Polonius or gracefully expound-ed by Lord Chesterfield, was not regarded as a set of take-it-or-leave-it tips for getting by in the world but as an agent of social evolution, the means by which one gener-ation could ensure a better future for the next.

What has changed so dramatically in the modern world is not the capacity or readiness of children to follow parental codes for living, but the difficulty of knowing any longer what those codes might be. Our current lives fail to provide the type of material from which we might construct the master scripts about how to live which were so readily available to our parents and grandparents.

This dilemma is perfectly captured in an encounter that forms the starting point for Richard Sennett's study of the personal consequences of work in the new capitalism, *The Corrosion of Character*. Sennett describes how he accidentally met the son of a man he had originally interviewed for an earlier book on blue-collar workers in America. Rico, he immediately observed, had done much better than his father. Whereas old Enrico had spent 20 years cleaning toilets and mopping floors in a downtown office building, Rico was one of life's new flexible workers, well-dressed, well-housed and regularly shifting homes and jobs as one lucrative contract came to an end and another beckoned.

Sennett remembered that Rico, as a boy, had resented the rules that his father had tried to impress upon him. But 'now that he is a father himself, the fear of a lack of ethical discipline haunts him'. What advice can he offer his own children? 'The objective example he could set, his upward mobility, is something they take for granted.' Neither is there anything in his working life that could stand as a moral guide, a parable about the best way to live. How can he emphasise the values that he still thinks important – formal obligation, trustworthiness, commitment and purpose – when his own life as a fully paid-up member of the new economy fails to provide any evidence of such long-term virtues?

We found many echoes of Rico's predicament in our own conversations. Fathers (and some mothers) generally agreed that there was little point in using their own social mobility as some sort of moral narrative for their children. As James the chemist had already intimated, children who took it for granted that they would roll off the examination conveyor-belt into university were not likely to extract much moral value from knowing about their own parents' struggle to achieve a similar goal.

As we've already intimated, it was fathers who most frequently lamented their diminishing ability to pass on anything of value to their children. Commentators on the changing role of the father, like Luigi Zola, go so far as to see this feeling of inadequacy as a possible factor in the increasing estrangement of modern fathers from their children. Fathers may not yet have been abolished, but they are certainly further away from their children than they ever were, and in many cases simply choose to step out of their lives. A father can no longer communicate with his children in cultural terms because of the pace of cultural change. He can't 'teach them his job, since the professions of his class shift... radically from decade to decade. He likewise finds it impossible to initiate his children into a social group, since another result of globalisation is an always increasing fluidity of the very society in which he moves; homes are frequently bought and sold as the family moves from one city or country to another; he can't teach values and principles to his children, since these grow too relative in the company of all the other shifts and changes'.

What, then, can parents hope to do for their children? What ambitions and hopes do they still feel it is realistic to entertain? Over and over again in our conversations we were told that what most concerned them was their children's eventual happiness. They didn't particularly care how this happiness was gained, whether from pursuing a specific career, championing a particular ideology or getting married to the perfect spouse. All that was far too prescriptive. They just wanted their children to be, well, happy. (It's interesting to find Scott Fitzgerald refusing to accept such vacuities from his own daughter. In 1933, he wrote to her: 'I am glad you are happy – but I never believe much in happiness. I never believe in misery either. Those are things that you see on the stage or screen or the printed page, they never really happen to you in life'.)

Is there anything more that contemporary middle-class parents can pass on to their children? There is always the family fortune. But it is increasingly difficult to regard the transmission of large impersonal sums of money to one's offspring with any sense of pride or satisfaction. If one knows that the money is going into the family business or into securing the family estate or into paying for one's child to pursue a distinctive vocation, then matters might be different. But the idea of handing over large sums of money to one's descendants without any knowledge of the uses to which it might be put (or any real sense that it might be genuinely needed) struck many of our conversationalists as peculiarly meaningless. There is also the suspicion that leaving over-generous legacies to one's children might be antisocial. In 2001, Bill Gates and a number of other leading industrialists united in a call to President Bush to abandon his ideas to reduce inheritance taxes on the grounds that the recipients of such increased sums would have little incentive to develop entrepreneurial skills of their own.

We are not, of course, suggesting that contemporary couples sit down and debate the loss of transmission narratives before deciding to remain childless. We are talking about the slow, cumulative creation of a climate of opinion in which the prospect of having children, particularly for the putative father, is becoming less attractive. Nobody has better captured this developing sense of paternal pointlessness than the renowned pessimist, Michel Houllebecq, in his novel *Atomised*:

Children existed solely to inherit a man's genes, his moral

code and his name. This was taken for granted among the aristocracy, but merchants, craftsmen and peasants also bought into the idea; it became the norm at every level of society. That's all gone now... there's nothing for my son to inherit. I have no craft to teach him, I haven't a clue what he might do when he's older. By the time he grows up, the rules I lived by will be meaningless – the world will be completely different. If a man accepts the fact that the world must change then his life is reduced to nothing more than the sum of his own experience – past and future generations mean nothing to him. That's how we live now. For a man to bring a child into the world now is meaningless.

So far we've been talking about inheritance stories almost solely with reference to children and parents. But we only need to go back a few decades to understand the way in which the arrival of a new child transformed far wider sets of relationships. In the days of the extended family, the decision to have children was prompted in a whole variety of ways by the emotional and physical proximity of one's own parents. Their evident desire for grandchildren, coupled with their assumption that this was part of the normal course of events in a family, were concrete factors to be taken into account in family planning. Not to have any children at all was to deny one's own parents the chance to play out roles that they almost regarded as their birthright. The immediate presence of parents also promised to relieve maternal anxieties during pregnancy as well as virtually guaranteeing the ready availability of enthusiastic childminders after the birth.

These traditionally taken-for-granted links between parents and grandparents (and more specifically between child-bearing daughter and mother) are still strong, but there is good evidence that they also are declining. The latest research shows that the proportion of women seeing their mothers once a week has significantly fallen since the Fifties. In 1986, 60 per cent of people with a non-resident mother saw her at least once a week: ten years later this figure had fallen to 49 per cent. The same decline was found between fathers and adult children. An optimistic gloss is sometimes placed on these figures by those who seek to champion the 'family of choice' against the biological family. Relations with immediate kin, we are told, may be sanctioned by tradition, but there is no reason at all to think them preferable to the sort of support that can be provided by close friends. But, unfortunately for this argument, there is no evidence that relatives are being replaced by friends. The proportion of people who saw their 'best friend' on a regular basis also fell during the period in which contacts with close relatives declined. 'It appears that people have generally become less likely to visit, or be visited by, anyone at all.' (McGlone, Park and Roberts).

Neither should we overlook wider kinship networks. It is not that long since aunts and uncles and cousins were significant people in our lives. The arrival of a new child reverberated throughout a network of relations. Such networks are becoming increasingly less important to younger generations. A recent survey showed, for example, that while more than half of those aged between 35-44 and two-thirds of those aged 55 and over agreed with the statement 'people should keep in touch with relatives like aunts, cousins and uncles, even if they don't have much in common', the figure in the case of 18-34-year-olds had fallen to four in ten.

In many of our discussions we detected a profound ambivalence about this new state of affairs. There was a strong feeling that one's own child was too personal and valued a possession to be shared with larger kinship networks which had nothing more than a biological connection to the new arrival. (In some cases, aunts and uncles only learned of their new kin when they spotted an additional name on a Christmas card!). But there were also times when the inability of members of the extended family to live up to expectations was a source of profound disappointment. One woman told us how upset she'd been to find that her parents showed only a perfunctory interest in her new child. They had no wish at all to become 'grandparents'. Not only did the very name uncomfortably remind them of their age, but they were also far too busy with their own immediate leisure and self-development projects to spend time on such unrewarding activities as looking after 'other people's children'. We met one 'grandmother' who was so eager to resist her traditional role that she retitled herself. She was not a 'granny' or a 'grandmother' but a 'second-generation parent'.

These developments not only have an impact on those with children, they also have serious implications for relatives who are childless. In the past, childless relations like the 'maiden aunt' could be regarded as figures who still had a social role to perform for those other members of their family with children. In today's world that role has receded in importance. Childlessness is no longer a state that can be attenuated by regular contacts with young nephews, nieces and cousins. It has become more of an absolute condition. This perhaps goes some way to explaining an apparent paradox. We live in a society in which more women than ever choose not to have children and yet also in which not being able to have children is seen as a personal tragedy and a major topic for scientific and public policy debate.

When we confronted parents with these sorts of

arguments about the place of their children within the extended family and the extent to which they might be regarded as their heirs, we sometimes found ourselves accused of being too analytical, too concerned with grand perspectives. People nowadays, we were told, had children for more intimate and interpersonal reasons. Couples explained that they decided to have children because it was one of the only ways in a world of ephemeral relationships, a world in which marriage had lost much of its meaning, that they could announce their own commitment, their only highly personal intention to stay together. They had at last found someone they wished to live with for a significant period of time, someone who could be counted on to be around during the complex, time-consuming business of child-rearing.

On the face of it, this might seem rather an admirable precondition for bringing children into the world. But it does depend upon what can only be described as a cavalier disregard of statistical evidence about family breakdown. How can individual couples feel confident that a child will bind them together when they are regularly confronted with figures showing that three out of ten children will now experience their parents divorcing before they have reached the age of 16? Cohabiting couples with children fare even worse. They are more likely to part than their married counterparts. We are fast approaching the point where only a minority of children will be born into a partnership that persists into their adulthood.

But surely people want to have children because there is something intrinsically fulfilling about the idea of bringing a child into the world? Nobody can say what the future might bring, but at least one can know that with a child in the family it will be possible to lay aside one's own selfish and material interests and find a unique pleasure in watching his or her development. People who haven't had children will never know the delight of hearing those first stuttered words, watching those first stumbling steps. Children allow us to rediscover the world. Their curiosity and imagination refresh our own tired perspectives. What could be more uplifting than watching your own offspring slowly make sense of the world through the stories that you tell them, the seaside and country outings that you arrange, the examples that you set?

We've no wish to deny the reality of such pleasures, but we don't have to look far to find parents who feel their traditional role of introducing their own children to the delights of the world is being undermined by the commercial market. Television and the Internet now offer even relatively young children a technicolor interactive introduction to life that can hardly be matched by the best efforts of even the most assiduous parents. Luigi Zoja provides the comparative perspective: 'For thousands of years, fathers taught their children how to ride a horse, and then, for a couple of generations, how to ride a bicycle. Today, the father has no authority when it comes to dealing with electronic games, and even his computer is different from those of his children. He belongs to a different world.'

These different worlds are even physically separated. Dozens of scientific studies have shown that children now spend more hours watching television and playing electronic games during their early years than upon any other activity. Personal testimonies reveal the degree of parental anxiety about the modern child's wish to remain alone in their own room for hours so that they can spend their time playing with the virtual technology that has now usurped traditional toys and pastimes. The latest figures suggest that 84 per cent of seven-to-ten-year-olds play video and computer games at home, and roughly 70 per cent of all children between nine and ten have a television in their bedroom. Parents who doubt the accuracy of these figures might ponder the modern paradox that one no longer sends a child to his or her room as a punishment. Nowadays the punishment is taking them out of their room!

These are serious concerns, but if we want to find out

the consequences of such shifts for the nature of childhood we need to consider the psychological and social effects of such extended exposure to electronic media. We need to consider the ways in which watching television doesn't merely inhibit the extent to which parents are able to introduce their own children to the mysteries of the world; it undermines it totally. As Joshua Meyrowitz writes in *No Sense of Place*:

> What is revolutionary about television is... that it allows the very young child to be 'present' at adult interactions... The widespread use of television is equivalent to a broad social decision to allow young children to be present at wars and funerals, courtships and seductions, criminal plots and cocktail parties.

These are not the only adult 'secrets' that television reveals. From situation comedies children also learn about the way in which adults play roles for them. Time after time, television parents are shown as behaving in one way in front of the children and in quite another way when they are alone. As Meyrowitz argues, this disrupts not only the notion of childhood but also that of parenthood:

> Television's exposure of the 'staging of childhood' – with its secret-keeping and the secret of secrecy – undermines both

traditional childhood naiveté *and* the all-knowing, confident adult role and fosters the movement toward a 'middle region' uni-age behavioural style.

Some might welcome such developments, in that they do at least promise to fatally subvert the 'innocence of childhood' myth that has been such a central part of our culture in the last century. Prospective parents, however, whose desire for children is at least partially prompted by the prospect of being able to introduce them to the wonders of the world, must increasingly face the fact that any such role has already been usurped. Times have changed for ever.

Very young children were once limited to the few sources of information available to them within or around the home: paintings, illustrations, views from a window, and what adults said and read to them. Television, however, now escorts children across the globe even before they have permission to cross the street. (Meyrowitz. p. 238).

It has not been our intention in this chapter to cite a list of reasons for not having children. As we said earlier, our concern is to demonstrate the manner in which many traditional and time-honoured accounts of raising a family have lost both their potency and their plausibility.

Our beliefs about the rising costs and risks of having children, however misinformed they might be, enjoy the cultural purchase that they do because of the lack of any counterbalancing stories. In the same way, our sense that having children now is diminished by the recognition that they will no longer, as in the past, be bearers of our occupations, beliefs and moral codes is given extra salience by the lack of fresh stories about those aspects of ourselves that they might carry forward into the future.

stories for children

Laurie. *You know, whenever you attack me for not having been a proper father, you always miss out on one dimension. I may not have pushed you in the way you now claim you would have liked, but I was at least optimistic about the sort of life that you might have. I was delighted that you were a member of a far more liberal and less repressed society than the one I'd endured as a teenager. I looked forward to seeing what you'd make of your life. I only wish I could detect that same sort of optimism when you talk about your own children.*

Matthew. *This is where we came in. Somehow kids no*

longer seem to fit the world as it is or the way we now think about ourselves. I can do the work, provide the care, pay the student fees, but it's a bit much to expect me to pretend that I'm always sure it's all worthwhile. That's one parental demand too many.

***

As we've seen, some of the most commonly cited reasons for not wanting children or for resenting their presence are based on shaky premises. The cost of having children does not appear to have risen in real terms, the risks to which they are exposed have not increased, the time we spend with them has expanded rather than shrunk. This suggests that something rather more important is going on than a mere shift in our attitudes to children. Our title question may be so difficult to answer because it is becoming, literally, unanswerable. We appear to be entering a unique period of history in which more and more people can no longer see the point of children. Children are not simply being planned, they are being actively avoided: they are becoming an expendable part of our existence.

This development is entirely a product of our new capacity to choose. Couples are no longer forced to have children because of the economic need for another breadwinner, or in order to ensure that they have someone who will be a source of support and comfort to them in their declining years. Neither are most modern women in industrialised societies propelled towards childbirth by powerful religious and cultural expectations. They are not prepared to accept their maternal role as biologically ordained. The universal and public stigma traditionally attached to women who chose to remain child-free or to content themselves with a single child or to bring up a child on their own, has, as we have seen, now become little more than a minority point of view. Neither are women forced to have children that are unintentionally conceived. Abortion and contraception make it possible for most to choose how many children they want, the time at which they wish to have them, and the possibility of remaining child-free for their whole life.

There are, of course, the extremely tragic examples of women who are unable to exercise these choices because they lack someone to father their child, or because of their own or their partner's infertility. And, of course, there are plenty of cases where people might decide that they have made the wrong choice, or where they feel, like the corporate women studied by Sylvia Ann Hewlett, that their eventual childlessness has been an example of 'creeping non-choice'. But even these exceptions hardly negate the proposition that an area of life that was once dominated by compulsion and necessity has now become a zone of free choice.

In the years before this state of affairs was realised there was widespread enthusiasm about its likely benefits. Women (and men), we were told, would be freed at last from the unnecessary pains of having children that they did not want and in many cases could not afford. Those who felt, for whatever reason, that they were unsuited to parenthood could happily find other forms of fulfilment. The prospects for the children born in this new age were regarded as particularly rosy. Our new-found ability to restrict the size of families would allow us to space our children's births in ways that were most conducive to their development and well-being. Every child would be a wanted child.

But, as we have shown throughout this book, our capacity to make choices about our children has by no means led to such general contentment. At the very time when we expected to be celebrating the type of fulfilled lives that would be made possible by this enlargement of choice, many of us find ourselves consumed by new doubts and uncertainties.

This is, perhaps, a sign of how much we have changed and of how far we still have to go. To put it at its simplest, our capacity to make our own rules and choices in this area has not yet grown to fill the vacuum created by the retreat of compulsion and tradition. The decline in the birth-rate and our ambivalence towards parenting are not straightforward consequences of the freedoms provided for us by contraception, abortion and the decline in religious and patriarchal authority. For if our current choices were freely and wisely made, then surely we would be happier with them.

What, then, has gone wrong? An important clue can be found in the suggestion by Schumpeter that the middle classes would eventually remain child-free because of their decision to bring to bear upon procreation the type of economic analysis that they had become so used to applying to so many other aspects of their lives.

This is a compelling argument. As citizens of capitalist societies, we are all used to thinking about our lives in terms of costs and benefits. We favour explanations and stories about other people's behaviour which make some sort of economic sense. It's a style of thinking that comes so naturally to us in most circumstances that we are inclined to characterise it as common sense. It has a moral compulsion.

But our attachment to this way of thinking, our commitment to what has been called 'economic rationality', can become a great source of frustration and unhappiness when it is applied to areas where it is inappropriate. This is the argument that lies at the heart of the Ralph Fevre's sweeping analysis of the problems of modern living, *The Demoralization of Western Culture*. What Fevre seeks to show is the way in which the ubiquity of economic rationality in our lives prevents us from imagining any 'alternative source of felicity'. Nowhere is this more evident than in the dilemmas we encounter in the area of childbirth and child-rearing. Instead of telling each other stories about the distinctive pleasures that can be derived from having children and watching them grow up, we fall back upon the economically based stories that inform so much of the rest of our existence and thereby come to regard our children as, at best, strangely disappointing and, at worst, pointless.

For Fevre, the perfect example of this approach can be seen in the parent, 'who, like the management guru, says it makes more sense to concentrate on what they are good at, can make more money doing, than to waste potential earning time on the care of their own children. In the jargon of corporate rationality the parent justifies the decision to "concentrate on their own business", and pay someone else – someone who is much better at doing this job, certainly more efficient at it – to look after their child.'

In our own enquiries we came across several examples of high-achieving couples who use such an array of paid care and careful time-planning that the periods in which both parents and children are actually together occupies only a tiny part of the week. As someone put it to us: 'I had Mark and Fiona over the other Sunday with their two young kids. It was quite obvious from the rows between them and the random nature of their supervision of the kids that this was an unusual and far from pleasant experience for both of them.' From the point of view of traditional morality this 'outsourcing' is quite obviously wrong-headed, but we cannot see this while we apply economic rationality to decisions which determine the sort of relationship we have with our children.

Even if we allow that many parents still believe their children have an intrinsic value that cannot ever be measured in such crude materialistic terms, we have to recognise the way in which the ubiquity of such stories about the cost of looking after them can produce an increasing sense of dissatisfaction.

Stories can have very powerful effects. As the American sociologist and political theorist, C. Wright Mills, pointed out long ago, our decision to act or not to act in a particular situation is much more readily explained by reference to the availability of viable cultural accounts or 'vocabularies of motive' than by recourse to lists of inner urges. What allows us to drive over the speed limit, consume dangerous drugs, or devote our lives to consumerism, is the knowledge that we can subsequently make sense of these actions to others by reciting culturally approved phrases and narratives. Culture, in the words of the anthropologist, Clifford Geertz, is no more than 'an ensemble of stories we tell about ourselves'.

What is urgently needed to balance the stories of the growing costs, sacrifices and risks of having children is a stronger and more plausible story about their uniquely non-economic benefits. Such a narrative would stress the manner in which having children and being involved in their upbringing provides a powerful sense of meaning in our own lives. It would not so much seek to reactivate the traditional and sentimental story about the wonders of children, but would talk of the way in which being with children and looking after them can absent us from our modern obsession with 'getting and spending' and offer a new and different opportunity for self-expression and fulfilment.

On the face of it, this narrative might seem self-indulgent in that it does not honour children in their own right but considers what being with them might do for us. History, though, cannot be reversed to a time when parenting came 'naturally'. Either we develop a self-regarding and reflexive account of parenting that is in tune with the times or we risk having no account at all.

At the same time, any such account would need to

counter the sense that children should always be proving their worth and value. This type of unreasonable expectation lies at the root of the concept of 'quality time'. Instead of allowing that there are times when we are merely with our children, or doing little else but attending to their immediate material needs, we seem to feel increasingly compelled to look for some positive, discernible outcome from our encounters.

The trouble is that, although parents know from hard experience that much of the time they spend with their children is inconsequential and boring, they are still inclined to regard this either as evidence of their own personal inadequacy or as a sign that their children are not coming up to the required standard. One father complained that the problem with children was that they could not, like so many other modern devices, simply be 'switched off' when they ceased to be entertaining and amusing. The desire for a more realistic story about the nature of life with young children can become overwhelming. In John O'Farrell's novel *The Best A Man Can Get*, such times with children are described as 'the tedium that dare not speak its name'. The hero announces: 'I want to come out of the closet and stand on top of the tallest climbing frame in the country and proclaim to the world, "Small children are boring".'

O'Farrell recognises that the courage to make any such

pronouncement can only come from a knowledge of out-comes. It is only possible to go on living with the knowledge that children are boring if one has a sense of what they might mean to one in the future. 'I now understand that having kids and raising a family was hard, because anything really worth achieving is hard.'

But this raises another difficulty. For, as we've already seen, the likelihood of parents regarding the raising of children as an achievement is imperilled by their inability to imagine the place that those children might take up in a future world. What is needed to remedy this situation is a story that would renew our confidence that there is a future world which our children will find full of exciting opportunities, opportunities that we can help them to realise. This was so much a part of the old parenting story that it has become a cliché. Postwar parents assumed that their children would not only do better than them, but would do so in a better world. In many ways their optimism was well placed: millions of parents in developed countries watched their child becoming the first in the family to enter higher education, to join a profession, to purchase their own home. They saw their children begin to benefit from advances in science and technology. Such parents found the pain of their own ageing alleviated by the vicarious pleasure of watching their children's expanding horizons.

Our own lack of a similarly compelling account of our own children's possible future is, no doubt, one of the key symptoms of our modern loss of faith in the notion of social progress. It goes hand in hand with the death of utopian ideals and the triumph of global capitalism. But we do not need to tackle such heady issues in order to remedy some of the present discontents about the value of parenting.

As we've seen, this feeling is partly generated by the manner in which the commonsense morality of 'getting and spending' generates an obsession with the present. As long as we are ceaselessly engaged in calculating our immediate sense of happiness and wellbeing, there is little space for thinking about our own lives in 20 years time, let alone the concrete future of our own children. But there is more to it than that.

'We are not suited to long perspectives,' wrote Philip Larkin, 'They link us to our losses.' The most fearsome of such losses is our own death, and in the last 50 years we have developed an extensive range of psychological devices for obscuring this brute fact. Death has, in Anthony Giddens' term, become 'sequestrated'. It is something to be hidden away, a slightly shameful matter that is best left to the professionals to handle. Death and the ensuing funeral once provided an opportunity for the coming together of far-flung members of the family and for a renewal of generational links. It was a time when the sons and daughters of the deceased could be solemnly reminded about their new importance within the family. It was the moment when they would come into their inheritance. But nowadays, in industrialised societies, even the death of a close relation is often little more than a temporary interruption, an event marked by a brisk cremation and a minimum period of mourning before everyone gets back to their own lives. Children, who once might have been expected to gain some sense of their place within an enduring family from attending the funeral of aunts and uncles and grandparents, are now likely to be excluded from such events altogether. In the words of Philippe Aries: 'Formerly children were told that they were brought by the stork, but they were admitted to the great farewell scene around the bed of the dying person. Today they are initiated in their early years into the physiology of love; but when they no longer see their grandfather and express astonishment, they are told that he is resting in a beautiful garden among the flowers.'

It is not difficult to see how this embarrassment about death inhibits any contemplation of the lives of future generations. Not thinking in any sort of detail about our own children's future is yet another way of obscuring our own mortality. Neither is there any indication that we atone for this lack of interest in the future by attending to past generations. Although millions of people now profess to an interest in their family history, it is significant that this is rarely a specific concern with the real day-to-day lives of their fathers and grandfathers or a precise curiosity about how they reared their children or how their aspirations for those children were fulfilled or not. Much more often this interest is a long-term historical enquiry, in which the chief pleasure comes from discovering one's biographical roots back 'in the mists of time'. This is using family to supplement our curriculum vitae, rather than as a means of providing some sense of living continuity between our closest relations. It is a telling insight into the modern familial condition that as we choose to spend less and less time with our proximate extended family, we become increasingly fascinated by our distant forebears.

The notion that we could do something to resolve some of our concerns about the meaning of children by finding ways to restore traditional family links is, of course, as idealistic as our other injunctions about the need to break the link between children and economic rationality. We make no apologies for this. There are, no doubt, a whole variety of concrete measures that could be taken to create a more 'family friendly' society, in which some of the current tensions associated with child-rearing could be alleviated without prompting cries of indignation from the determinedly childless. But we do not imagine that any such tinkering could resolve the ways of thinking that lie at the root of so much current sadness and uncertainty.

Consider the questions that we raised earlier about the costs of children. Our review of government policies aimed at reducing such costs shows them to have been remarkably unsuccessful. This is hardly surprising. As long as our guiding principles involve maximising income, expanding consumption, and a narrow notion of self-development, it is difficult to see how government could ever hope to compensate fully for the sacrifices involved in having children. How could any government manage to offset the 'costs' incurred by parents who find child-rearing incompatible with their desire for self-realisation on a three-month trip to Tibet?

This is why we have called for new accounts or stories about child-rearing that provide an antidote to current ways of thinking. The emergence of such stories (and we have only tried to sketch their content) can only occur when the 'secrets' that parents and non-parents now tell about their discontents become public – recognised as symptoms of a general cultural malaise rather than evidence of personal failings. We can only hope that this book contributes to that 'coming out', that it helps to facilitate what Robert Bellah and his colleagues in *Habits of the Heart* have called 'public philosophy', a readiness to engage in a form of reflection and discourse that helps us to 'make connections that are not obvious and to ask difficult questions'. Any such public debate must take into account the way in which procreation is related to tomorrow's major political and social questions. It is to this task that we now turn.

children of the future

Matthew. *I remember that when I first asked you talk about your reasons for having me, you were reluctant to do anything more than shrug your shoulders and talk in your usual fatalistic way about the generation gap being a fact of life that I should learn to live with. But the longer we went on talking, the more you seemed ready to admit that our disagreements weren't merely personal but had something to do with problems that existed for many parents and children in our age. You almost seemed ready to talk about possible solutions.*

Laurie. *Well, having spent the best part of two decades being told by you that everything you didn't like in the world was directly caused by Thatcherism or capitalism, or that everything you didn't like about yourself was caused by me or your mother, there didn't seem much point in debating the finer points of social ills. Maybe it's because you've become less of a determinist that I'm more willing to talk to you about how the world might be changed for the better.*

***

What are children for? In this short book we have repeatedly suggested that this is a question we are all finding more and more difficult to answer. It seems that if we are to enjoy and appreciate our children as parents and as a society we need new stories about their meaning and significance. But there is another step to take. We cannot leave the subject of children and their place in the world without considering some of the recent developments which look likely to influence the debate about child-bearing and child-rearing in the years to come.

Progress in science and medicine may not be sufficient on its own to explain the changes in our attitudes to children but it is certainly necessary. Reliable contraception, safe abortion and the decline in infant mortality have all played their part in shifting traditional beliefs about the value and the meaning of children. New developments in fertility treatment and in our capacity to manipulate genetic inheritance now seem set to transform the biological context once again. Beckoning us into the future are the wrinkled hands of geriatric mothers and the perfect smiles on the perfect faces of their designer babies.

Our faith in the, as yet, largely unfulfilled promises of the fertility treatment industry is already shaping lives. Sylvia Ann Hewlett found that many in her sample of successful young women had decided not to have children in their twenties on the assumption that fertility advances would enable them to choose to become mothers well into middle age. It will surely not be long before men and women are deciding to postpone child-bearing until the time arrives when they can genetically ensure that their offspring will be free from physical defects.

Given the apparent speed and scale of scientific advance, it is hardly surprising that accounts of the future are often characterised by technological determinism, by a belief that science can be counted on to fulfil its promises and that there is little that humans can do but stand by and let it takes its course. This is a dangerous perspective. We may easily become so enamoured by the power of science to remove the biological constraints that once controlled childbirth that we ignore the other equally important constraints that still underpin social attitudes.

It is not for us to say that there is a good or a bad time to have children. Each person will be different, the energy and dynamism of the youthful parent can be contrasted with the wisdom and maturity of an older generation. But until science liberates us from mortality itself, we need to consider the social consequences of late parenting. It is obvious, for example, that the older the parent the smaller the proportion of their children's lives they are likely to share. This book is itself evidence of the way in which a relationship between a father and son can continue to grow and develop 40 years from its beginning. More specifically, there seems to be a particular heightening of empathy (or potential for such heightening) which occurs when a grown-up child approaches the age that their parents were at their birth. This overlapping of life stories is given even more depth and texture by the arrival of the next generation. One need not share Freud's mordant observation that the reason grandchildren and grandparents get on so well is that 'they share a common enemy' to recognise how the coexistence of three (and in some cases four) generations brings new possibilities of support, fascination and fulfilment to all concerned.

None of this is meant to judge or to condemn older parents. But thinking again of Sylvia Ann Hewlett's young subjects, we might question whether (even if their faith in fertility advances proves to be well grounded) they are really happy in their choice. Can we truly be said to have our priorities properly ordered when we place career advancement and income maximisation over the possibility of enjoying an active relationship not only with adult children, but also with grandchildren or even great-grandchildren? One plausible answer to the question 'what are children for' is surely 'to grow into adult friends, and to give us the pleasure of being grandparents'? It is a strange kind of liberation that 'frees' us from these possibilities.

Similar social and moral questions are raised by the genetic revolution. Obviously, we celebrate the possibility that genetics can tackle inherited disorders and predispositions to disease. But increasingly many of us also seem resigned to the very different prospect of parents seeking to manipulate 'normal' genetically transmitted characteristics in pursuit of the 'perfect' baby.

The boundary between genetic disorder and mere parental preference is ambiguous. In a world where we can buy pretty much anything we want, the way we want it, off the shelf, it is increasingly easy to conflate quite different kinds of genetic manipulation: to make little distinction between the parents who try to ensure that their next child will not inherit a life-threatening or serious disease and those who might seek to 'play God' by genetically imbuing their next child with such 'favourable' psychological assets as high intelligence or lack of shyness.

Of course, both in our choice of partner and in the way we socialise our children we may seek to shape our children's future. But our selection of partner is a choice about our own lives not that of our offspring. And however we choose to socialise our children we cannot remove their capacity to reject our advice and aspiration. Both decisions are thus categorically different from determining (or seeking to determine) the IQ or degree of extroversion that our children will carry with them from the cradle to the grave.

Yet while seeking to determine our children's characteristics is an unwarranted infringement of their right to be the subject of their own life (and one for which they surely will not thank us), it is also, in an important sense, futile. The moral aesthetic of our lives concerns the way we carve our own unique history from the raw material and the tools we are handed by our inheritance, our circumstances and fate. Our task as parents is to create the raw material and to teach our children as best we can how to use the tools, it is not to try to carve out the shape of that life before it has even begun. 'What are children for?' They are for being who they (not we) uniquely are, for living their own lives, for creating their *own* stories.

The irony of the deterministic (and generally fearful)

public discourse about genetic manipulation is that this science could provide a powerful basis for renewing parenting narratives. Faith in God and visions of heavenly paradise may have lost their hold, but our new appreciation of our genetic legacy can provide an alternative source of immortality. We know now with a certainty we have never had before that our parental efforts can be inspired not only by a combination of love and duty, but also by the knowledge that our genetic imprint will always be an essential part of our successors' distinctive perspective on a new and possibly better world.

'Till Death Do Us Part?'

We can also confidently forecast that the debate about families and children will continue to be bound up with fierce arguments about the effects of single parenthood, separation and divorce. Despite a huge and growing volume of research the evidence in this area is at best ambiguous and at worst downright contradictory. In January 2002, the *Observer* reported the work of E. Mavis Hetherington, professor emeritus at the University of Virginia. Professor Hetherington's research over 25 years suggests that the vast majority of children whose parents divorce suffer no long-term damage at all. Yet, as the newspaper reminded its surely bemused readers, these findings directly contradicted the conclusions which had previously been reached in another 'comprehensive' study by Californian professor Judith Wallerstein.

We take a more modest position than those who see the decline of lifelong marriage as either disastrous or as a cause for celebration. Until 30 years ago, those who left a failing marriage or sought to bring up a child alone were breaking with the prevailing conventions of society and risked being looked on with a mixture of pity and contempt. But now, approaching the time when only a minority of children will be born and live their entire childhood with their birth parents, different conventions and norms hold sway. When we are no longer satisfied with living in one place or with having one career, why should we continue to persist with the ideal of having one partner? Yet can we really say that the new freedom we have to abandon relationships when they become difficult and constraining is making us more content?

The most pressing priority for family policy is surely to give the poorest in our society the reason to hope for their children's future. But, in fending off those who would punish or stigmatise the non-conventional family, we should also recognise the need for narratives that celebrate persistence as well as change, consistency as well as autonomy, depth of experience as well as range.

Stories about the effect of children upon marriages tend to be overridingly negative. Here, for example, is Susan Maushart, author of *Wifework: What Marriage Really Means for Women*: 'There is something absurd about the notion that children are bad for marriages. Yet, absurd or not, it is an undeniable part of the social reality in which we are mired.'

This is a short-term view. In our discussions we were often struck by stories of couples who freely admitted the pressures on them in the early years of parenting but who now felt that they had come 'out the other side'. As their children move on into adulthood, these couples can 're-discover' each other, enjoying the fruits of affluence but secure in the knowledge that they have fulfilled their contract to each other and their children. Not all of us can achieve this state, but as we confront the constraints and pressures of long-term commitment and parenting we should feel able to draw on these narratives.

Of course, for some, the very necessity of even embarking on an adult relationship is questionable. It is clear that many single mothers bring up their children successfully, despite the pressures they face. It also appears that more middle-class women are choosing the path of lone parenthood. In *Wifework*, Susan Maushart extols the virtues of her own status as a single mother and suggests that many other women will follow her choice:

Women still seek husbands in order to provide fathers for their children. But, rightly or wrongly they are doing so with significantly reduced urgency, and acutely heightened ambivalence.

Maushart's rhetoric chimes with the demographic evidence from Mediterranean countries, indicating the correlation between the decline in fertility and the persistence of unequal gender roles in the home. Although men have started to take on more work in the home, women continue to shoulder a greater burden in terms of career sacrifices, childcare and domestic labour. For those who believe that – all things being equal – two parents are better than one, the answer is not to attack single mothers. It is to recognise that being a modern father means a greater willingness to negotiate ambitions, to resist temptations and to tackle the housework. For, as much research has found, one of the main consequences of childbirth for the modern egalitarian couple is the re-emergence of traditional gender roles.

race and identity

As we explained earlier, the decline in fertility in many developed nations will necessitate major increases in inward migration if those countries are to staff public services and provide for an ageing population. This offers a new impetus to right-wing pro-natalism. For men like Patrick Buchanan, the decline in the fertility of indigenous whites threatens their eventual decline into minority status. This is dangerous territory.

There is an urgent need for political leaders to prepare their populations for the inevitable increase in immigration resulting from both push (hunger, war, oppression) and pull (the need for labour) factors. Unless they do so, conflict between the economic need for migrants and the social resistance to greater diversity could become the defining and destructive obsession of the first decades of the 21st century. The simple message we must learn is that greater migration and multiethnicity is not an option to be promoted or resisted, it is an inevitability to which we must find ways of adjusting. Making multiethnicity work is a personal as well as a political challenge.

In the postwar decades parents could bring their children up with a set of norms, beliefs and values, knowing that these would be broadly shared by the other adults their children would meet. Now, our own children (grandchildren) live in a borough of London where 130 languages are spoken, attend a primary school where whites are in a minority and where those with parents born in the UK are a bare majority. The other day nine-year-old Joseph explained that his best friend couldn't come out to play football 'because he has his Muslim lesson on Saturday mornings'.

Despite the scale of global inequality and injustice and the many obstacles to progress, children being born now really can be history's first global citizens. Those who grow up and are encouraged to feel at home in neighbourhoods that are themselves microcosms of the global mix will be at a distinct advantage. In our connected world of complex interactions and services, those who have from early on learned how to deal with, understand and respect social and cultural difference will grow up with the building-blocks of what will arguably be the generic skills of the new century – those of the social entrepreneur.

But the advantages and pleasures of growing amid diversity are rarely heard above the relentless tide of stories of inner-city crime, collapsing public services and crime- and drug-ravaged schools. Of course, some state schools (including, it should be said, many in all-white areas) are so disastrous it seems almost negligent to send children to them. But with parental support, bright kids tend to succeed whatever the environment. By withdrawing children into the seclusion of a relatively homogeneous private education, affluent suburbs or gated estates, parents are underestimating their children's resilience and the individual and social benefits of growing up in a multiethnic community.

We live in dangerous times, where both the political right and separatist radicals have an easy and powerful script. Preparing our children for enthusiastic participation in a shrinking world and in their own multiethnic neighbourhoods is a vital task for today's and tomorrow's parents.

work, wealth and progress

In the Sixties and Seventies we became used to predictions of the end of work. Our growing confidence in the power of the silicon chip and our loss of confidence in the capacity of the state and the market to create full employment led to the widespread view that we faced a future of lifetime unemployment for the many and lifetime leisure for the lucky few. How wrong we all were. In early 2002, for example, came further research evidence of rising working hours in the UK, along with the news that the days of early retirement are over and that it may well be time to consider raising the statutory retirement age. Alongside all of this there is the continuing rise of female employment, which means that in countries like the USA and UK the total employed hours of the average family have risen dramatically over the last three decades.

No wonder that the agenda for improving the lot of parents is dominated by the need to reduce working hours and allow parents to better balance home and work. Despite the unthinking opposition of employer organisations and the churlish hostility of some non-parents, most of us support the demand for more 'family-friendly' work. But we must also recognise that the problem does not just lie in inflexible businesses or weak employment laws. The simple – although uncomfortable – fact is that millions of middle-class people work long hours not because they are compelled to but because they choose to.

The intrusive nature of modern work lies not only in the long-hours culture (reversing the previous century of falling weekly hours) but in the changing nature of work. More and more employees are required to travel as part of their work, to be available all the time through mobile phone, bleeper or e-mail, to accept workloads that cut across the routines and expectations of family life. But perhaps even more invasive are the core values of modern work brilliantly captured by Richard Sennett in his book *The Corrosion of Character*.

Sennett describes the unbalanced contract of modern work in which the employee is expected to give more time, commitment, more indeed of his very identity. But instead of this being underpinned by feelings of continuity and loyalty (to company, place or class), it is marked by the experience of insecurity, insincerity, attenuation of identity. We give more and more of ourselves to work and get less and less in return. What work gives us back makes the rest of our lives even harder to handle.

Yet the living standards of the average family in the advanced economies continue to rise rapidly. In the last chapter we explored how new stories about bringing up children might subvert the powerful logic of economic rationality. But there are more prosaic ways in which we might seek to provide relief from the conviction that we must keep on working ever harder despite what such work is doing to our own lives. As long as we go on believing that the fulfilment of our needs relies upon income maximisation, the more we will feel that our moral duty to our children is to work as hard and earn as much as we can, and the more we will resent the manner in which their presence forecloses our opportunities for consumerism.

One part of the remedy is old-fashioned: we need strong public services and decent benefit levels. If we and our children could confidently rely upon good public health and education services as well as the provision of safe, free, and exciting public spaces and opportunities for sport and cultural participation, we might be less susceptible to the call of the market to engage in ceaseless earning and consumption.

This argument is given interesting new support by research undertaken by Yew-Kwan Ng of the University of Hong Kong, which demonstrates that increasing the proportion of national resources on public spending is an efficient way of raising happiness levels in advanced economies.

We are suggesting, then, that a new public philosophy that drives economic reasoning away from such inappropriate regions as child-bearing, coupled with the provision of strong public services, might go some way to resolve the dilemmas cited in this book by parents and non-parents. But we are saying something else as well. The very way in which we bring up our children can also be a vital way of discovering forms of happiness that lie outside income accumulation and consumerism. Most parents yearn to rear their children in such a way as to ensure that they develop a capacity to build strong relationships, to fulfil their responsibilities to society, and to find eventual happiness. But this is only another source of parental feelings of inadequacy. For although they may have such wishes for their children, they are hardly in a position to act as a role model when in their own lives they only appear as workaholics relying upon material consumption to compensate themselves and their children for the strains and anxieties of modern living. Ralph Fevre elegantly captures the paradox:

Parents argue over whose work is more important, meaning who (usually the man) is going to be permitted to follow the diktat of the sham morality most closely, but a real morality would have them discussing whose turn it was to have the great privilege of looking after their own children.

It could, of course, be the case, that by manifesting our own exhaustion, emotional fragility and confusion, we are giving our children powerful reasons to rebel against us and to demand a more human-centred order of things. But surely it would be better to work with rather than against our children; better for them to feel that they have picked up the baton from us as they pursue a way of life and a social structure in which human fulfilment and happiness have supplanted GDP growth and acquisition as our ultimate goals.

last words

By Matthew Taylor

Writing this little book has been a personal adventure, an opportunity to work with my father that has had a very different feel from a past adult relationship based on the too easy currency of beer, curry and football. Although we are both hardworking and reasonably successful in our chosen (and increasingly converging) careers, I don't suppose either of us would put risk-taking or doggedness at the top of a list of our attributes. Yet, at times, writing the book has felt very risky indeed, principally because of its possible impact on our relationship.

We have spent more time at close quarters and certainly more concerted time talking with each other than ever before. There have been moments when – however hard we might have tried to disguise it – we have questioned each other's commitment to the project; when we have become irritated by what we variously saw as stubborn modes of thinking, ideological inconsistency and special pleading. But, having assumed and acted upon the assumption that there was a certain fragile and brittle quality to our relationship, we have put it under strain and been pleasantly surprised at its resilience. Speaking to my own friends – many of whom feel they are very remote from their fathers – I have been struck by how envious they are of this opportunity.

As Laurie said in his 'first words', part of the inspiration for this book came from the feelings of frustration and inadequacy that I was experiencing within a conventional and apparently functional family. The frustrations continue. I have no doubt I will carry on to fall short of many people's mark for a proper family man. But writing the book has been therapeutic. It has enabled me to understand why my own commitments sometimes feel so onerous: it has helped me at least to recognise the victim's script of 'costs and burdens'. It has made me better able to recognise the paradox that what is most important and even rewarding about family life is precisely its open-ended, indeterminate, messy nature. I haven't stopped working too hard; I haven't stopped getting tired and irritated with my boys; I can't claim to have done much more housework, but maybe I have become a slightly more laid-back, more contented – one might even say 'more fatherly' – father.

Something else has been going on. In this book we have examined how constant striving and voracious consuming are difficult to reconcile with having kids. They are also difficult to reconcile with a balanced life. This is especially true as we get older: the work gets harder, we tot up the ambitions that will remain unfulfilled, and realise that even some aspects of consumption are losing their appeal. We are approaching the crossroads identified by Eric Erickson at which we take the route of resignation or remorse. As ageing forces us to face up to the pathos of life (for if we don't we are doomed to becoming ridiculous or mad), family comes into its own. This is not just true of parents and grandparents but can be so for step-parents, uncles, aunts, close family friends. Family can provide those narratives of continuity, transmission, and even immortality that compensate for the more transient pleasures of money, success, and romantic love.

For many of us the idea of family is associated with the mundane in contrast to the ambitions and rewards of our professional lives. Yet, in a world of constant change, a brutal meritocracy, in which the winners take all and the losers are made to feel inadequate and worthless, the family is not only a zone of comfort but can also be a place of authenticity. If ultimately our greatest ambition is to find some enduring sense of meaning to our existence, we are as likely to find that in our family life as anywhere. Writing this book has not provided me with answers to the big questions life poses, but at least it now feels as though I've begun to look in the right direction.

references

Aries, Philippe. *Western Attitudes Towards Death*. Johns Hopkins University Press. 1990

Bellah, R.N.; Madsen, R.; Swidler, A.; Sullivan, W.M.; Tipton, S.M. *Habits of the Heart*. University of California Press. 1990

Betjeman, John. *Summoned by Bells*. John Murray. 1997

Buchanan, Patrick. *The Death of the West*. St Martin's Press. 2001

Burkett, Elinor. *The Baby Boon: How Family-Friendly America Cheats the Childless*. The Free Press. 2000

Cook, Dan. 'Lunch-box hegemony, kids and the marketplace'. *LiP Magazine*. August 21st. 2001

Crittenden, Anne. *The Price of Motherhood*. Henry Holt. 2001

Erickson, Eric. *Childhood and Society*. Norton. 1963

Falbo, Toni. *The Single Child Family*. Guilford Press. 1984

Fevre, R.W. *The Demoralization of Western Culture*. Continuum. 2001

Francis-Cheung, Theresa. *Help Yourself Cope with Your Biological Clock*. Hodder & Stoughton. 2001

Furedi, Frank. *Paranoid Parenting*. Allen Lane. 2001

Hewlett, Sylvia Ann. *Creating a Life: Professional Women and the Quest for Children*. Talk Miramax Books. 2002

Hewlett, Sylvia Ann and West, Cornell. *The War Against Parents*. Scott Schaffer. 1998

Houllebecq, Michel. *Atomised*. Heinemann. 2000

Hrdy, Sarah. *Mother Love: Evolution and the Maternal Instinct.* Chatto. 1999

Maushart, Susan. *Wifework*. Bloomsbury. 2002

Meyrowitz, Joshua. *No Sense of Place*. Oxford University Press. 1985

Middleton, S.; Ashworth, K.; Braithwaite, I. *Small Fortunes: Spending on Children, Childhood Poverty and Parental Sacrifice.* Joseph Rowntree Foundation. 1997

Mills, C.Wright. *Character and Social Structure*. Harcourt. 1990

Oakley, Ann. *Becoming a Mother*. Martin Robertson. 1979
O'Farrell, John. *The Best A Man Can Get*. Doubleday. 2001

Schumpeter, Joseph. *Capitalism, Socialism and Democracy*. Harper and Row. 1983

Scraton, Phil. *Childhood in Crisis*. Taylor and Francis. 1996

Sennett, Richard. *The Corrosion of Character*. Norton, W.W. & Company. 1999

Wallerstein, J.; Blakeslee, S.; Lewis, J. *The Unexpected Legacy of Divorce*. Hyperion. 2000

Wattenburg, Ben. *The Birth Dearth. What Happens When People in Free Countries Don't Have Enough Babies?* 1987

Zoja, Luigi. *The Father: Historical, Psychological and Cultural Perspectives.* 2001